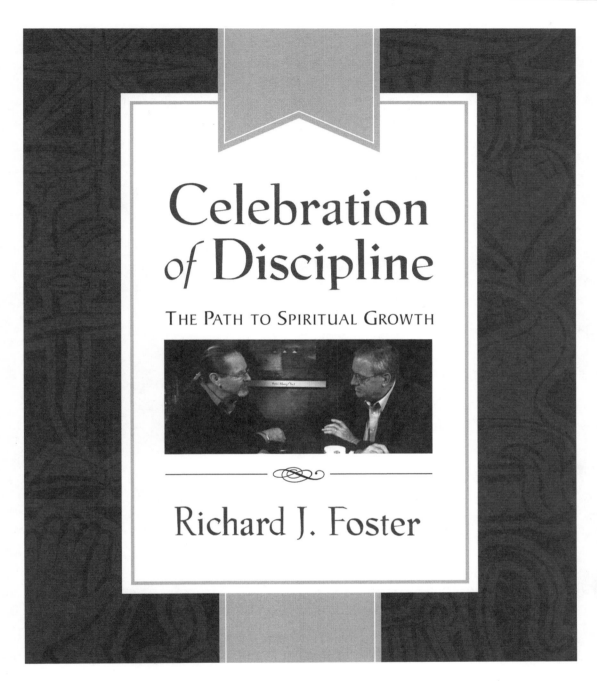

Celebration of Discipline

THE PATH TO SPIRITUAL GROWTH

Richard J. Foster

LEADER'S GUIDE

BOOKS BY RICHARD J. FOSTER

- *Celebration of Discipline: The Path to Spiritual Growth*
- *Celebrating the Disciplines (with Kathryn A. Yanni)*
- *The Challenge of the Disciplined Life*
- *Devotional Classics (edited with James Bryan Smith)*
- *Freedom of Simplicity*
- *Prayer: Finding the Heart's True Home*
- *Prayers From the Heart*
- *Richard J. Foster's Study Guide for Celebration of Discipline*
- *Seeking the Kingdom*
- *Spiritual Classics (edited with Emilie Griffin)*
- *Streams of Living Water*

BOOKS BY GARY W. MOON/OTHER RESOURCES

Multimedia Curriculum *(Curriculum of Christlikeness Series)*

- *God Views: Seeing Clearly the One Who Loves You Most*
- *Renovation of the Heart*

Family Devotion/Children's Curriculum

- *The Bible Ride: Adventures That Bring the Gospel to Life (Volumes 1-4)*
- *The Bible Ride Atlas (Volumes 1-4)*
- *The Bible Ride Scenic Route (Volumes 1-4)*

Also by the Author:

- *Homesick for Eden: A Soul's Journey to Joy*
- *Falling for God: Saying Yes to His Extravagant Proposal*
- *Spiritual Direction and the Care of Souls: A Guide to Christian Approaches and Practices (edited by Gary W. Moon and David G. Benner)*

To Contact the Publisher:

Web: www.lifesprings.net
Phone: 1.800.541.1376
Address: LifeSprings Resources
           2425 West Main Street
           P.O. Box 9
           Franklin Springs, GA 30639-0009

CELEBRATION OF DISCIPLINE

THE PATH TO SPIRITUAL GROWTH

LEADER'S GUIDE

GARY W. MOON

Requests for information should be addressed to:

LifeSprings Resources
P.O. Box 9
Franklin Springs, GA 30639

ISBN: 1-932776-02-8

Written by Gary W. Moon
Designed by Jeffrey Hayes Johnson

Printed in the United States of America

Contents

Introduction

What makes a book a classic? Is it the number of readers? If so, *Celebration of Discipline* should qualify. Since its publication in 1978, it has been read by approximately two million people and translated into dozens of languages.

Yes, but what about critical acclaim as the most important barometer? *Celebration of Discipline* has been cited by many as the best modern book on Christian spirituality and praised by *Christianity Today* as one of the ten best books of the twentieth century.

Still unconvinced? Listen to this: A panel of acclaimed writers and critics were wrestling with this same question (What makes a book a classic?) on Radio National's program *Book Talk*. After much debate, the panel proposed that perhaps the best definition was this: "A classic is a book that has never finished saying what it's got to say."

That's the best test. And every time I see a cluster of young people—who were not even born when *Celebration of Discipline* was first released—passing around copies of Foster's text, I know that this classic test has been passed. *Celebration of Discipline* has jumped a generation. It is a book that may never be finished with what it has to say.

Why? Why is this book so important?

I believe it begins with the inspiration of the title. The notion of celebrating instead of dreading a disciplined life is enough to make you crack the cover. And once you look inside, you discover that Richard Foster mined spiritual treasures that were buried and unavailable to most modern Protestant Christians. But finding this trove would not have been enough. Foster is an artful storyteller whose prose often borders on the poetic. His descriptions are artistic and alive. He has not only found rare treasure, but he makes you want to let it pour through your own fingers, to experience his words.

Celebration of Discipline is written in a style that is warm, inviting, and very respectful of each great tributary of Christian spirituality. It is written by someone very skillful in separating the wheat from the chaff—presenting what is most important with great conservation of words.

Richard Foster is also a master of organization. In *Celebration of Discipline* he has divided twelve prominent Christian Disciplines into three movements of the Spirit: inward (meditation, prayer, fasting, and study), outward (simplicity, solitude, submission, and service) and corporate (confession, worship, guidance, and celebration).

Last but not least, Foster offers a wealth of examples demonstrating how the Christian Disciplines can become woven into the fabric of daily life.

Richard J. Foster is a practical mystic, a poetic scholar, and an evangelist of transformation. It is no wonder his most famous book has become so cherished. *Celebration of Discipline* illuminates the path to spiritual growth, and will do so for generations to come.

THIS KIT CONTAINS

Celebration of Discipline DVD

A thirteen-part video series that features Richard J. Foster presenting summaries of each chapter of *Celebration of Discipline*, followed by an unscripted conversation over coffee between Richard and Dallas Willard. Also featured are the music of George Skramstad and Jim Stewart and informative interactions with Glandion Carney and Margaret Campbell.

Leader's Guide

A comprehensive guide providing all the information you will need for leading your group through the thirteen sessions of the course. The guide is also flexible. If group discussion goes overtime, you may assign other parts of the lesson plan as homework assignments.

Participant's Guide

Contains questions and exercises for each session and is designed to help participants process the material with both heads and hearts. We start with the assumption that the participants will not have studied the lesson prior to class. The exercises do not require any pre-class work to be effective.

We do hope, however, that the class will inspire the participants to some post-class study and practice with the particular Spiritual Discipline covered in the group meeting. Participants are encouraged to read the corresponding chapter from *Celebration of Discipline* before attending each group session.

CD-ROM

This CD-ROM contains promotional materials, teaching outlines, and a transcript of conversation between Richard J. Foster and Dallas Willard.

Additional kits and copies of the Leader's Guide and Participant's Guide are available from:

LifeSprings Resources
P.O. Box 9
2425 West Main Street
Franklin Springs, GA 30639
www.lifespringsresources.com/celebration

How This Leader's Guide Is Organized

This Leader's Guide is divided into thirteen sessions (lessons). Each 45- to 60-minute session involves an integration of a section of the *Celebration of Discipline* DVD with material presented in the Leader's Guide and Participant's Guide.

For each session *the leader* will need:

- Leader's Guide
- Bible
- DVD Player, Monitor, Stand, Extension Cord, etc.
- *Celebration of Discipline* DVD
- *Celebration of Discipline* (the book)

For each session *the participant* will need:
- Bible
- Participant's Guide
- Pen or Pencil

Each session is divided into eight parts:

- Before You Lead
- Introduction
- Warm-Up
- DVD
- Bible Study
- Transforming Exercises
- Summary
- Appendix

Each part is explained in detail on the next two pages.

BEFORE YOU LEAD

Before the lesson itself, you will be presented with a brief overview that will include important quotes, Scripture reference, list of materials needed, and the session outline. All you need to be an effective group leader is contained within this packet and between your ears. However, you and the group participants are encouraged to read or reread the corresponding chapter from *Celebration of Discipline* before class each week.

■ Quotes
Quotes from *Celebration of Discipline* and other RENOVARÉ resources are provided as a way to focus each session.

■ Scripture Reference
A verse or verses of Scripture are provided to underscore how each Discipline is tied to the biblical text.

■ Materials
The materials listed are important for both leader and participants. The corresponding chapter from *Celebration of Discipline* will be listed here.

■ Session Outline
This is an at-a-glance overview of the content and activities to be covered during the session.

THE SIX-PART SESSION

❶ Introduction
Includes calling the class together with a brief welcome and opening prayer. The prayer will typically be taken from Richard J. Foster's *Prayers From the Heart*.

❷ Warm-Up

■ Overview and Illustration
The warm-up time may include a story or the retelling of an illustration found in *Celebration of Discipline*. These stories or illustrations are presented as a synopsis of a central teaching point for the lesson.

■ **Corresponding Freedom**
The corresponding freedom associated with each Discipline will be listed here for thought and discussion.

■ **Homework**
While participants are not required to complete homework assignments, you are advised to create some space for discussion of outside readings (i.e., the corresponding chapter from *Celebration of Discipline*).

③ DVD

The majority of class time is focused on the video content, through which you will guide the students. This will include viewing the video vignette (and the short "bonus" section if you choose), followed by discussion. Suggested reflection questions are provided.

④ Bible Study

A Bible study is provided for each lesson. There is a copy in the Leader's Guide and in the Participant's Guide. The Bible study also includes suggested daily Scripture readings.

⑤ Transforming Exercises

A *Small Group Exercise* will be suggested, and *Individual Exercises* for homework will be listed. The homework suggestions correspond to the five components of the person—thought, emotion, will, behavior, and social interactions.

⑥ Summary

Richard's Recommendations
In this section Richard will provide a suggestion for additional readings—one old and one new.

Other RENOVARÉ Resources
Suggestions for further study from RENOVARÉ resources are listed here.

APPENDIX

In the appendix you will find reproductions of the exercises that appear in the Participant's Guide. These include:

- *Bible Study*
- *Small Group Exercise*
- *Individual Exercises*

The appendix also includes a Teaching Outline for the leader.

BEFORE THE FIRST SESSION

The *Celebration of Discipline* curriculum is designed to be user-friendly. We know it is the rare teacher who has several hours each week to prepare for leading class. We suggest the following preparation (probably less than one hour of your time):

1 Review lesson outline and exercises in the appendix section.

2 Watch the appropriate video segment and have DVD cued for class.

3 Make sure there will be enough pens or pencils for the participants.

4 Familiarize yourself with the standard structure of presentation (see above).

5 Read through the Leader's Guide for the lesson, and use the margins for notes.

UNIQUE FEATURES

1 No requirements for students before coming to class—although they should be encouraged to read the corresponding chapters from *Celebration of Discipline*.

2 Homework and additional readings for students who become inspired during class and want to go further.

3 More material than you will need—exercises can become homework.

4 The leader is more of a facilitator than a verse-by-verse teacher.

5 Flexibility concerning presentation style (e.g., you may use a small-group or large-group format for discussion and use of exercises).

TIPS FOR LEADING GROUP DISCUSSION

1 Allow group members to participate at their own comfort levels. Not everyone need answer every question.

2 Ask questions with interest and warmth, and then listen carefully to individual responses. Remember: No answer is too insignificant. Encourage and affirm each person's participation.

3 Be flexible: Reword questions if necessary. Take the liberty of adding or deleting questions to accommodate the needs of your group.

And speaking of flexibility, whenever discussion times are teeming with life, do not feel obligated to complete the entire session plan. As a rule of thumb, good discussion beats a structured lesson, but the recommended structure beats lifeless discussion. Again, flexibility and sensitivity are the keys. Any of the exercises can become homework assignments if the group becomes pressed for time due to helpful and energetic discussion.

4 Ask for (and expect) differences of opinion and experience.

5 Don't be afraid of silence. Allow people time to think. Digestion takes time.

6 Never force someone to disclose homework or journaling activities. In fact, assure them up front that such disclosure will never be required.

7 Many items in your session notes (particularly those labeled "Question," "Exercise," and "Discussion") are written in second person to allow the leader to read these words directly to the participants.

8 Allow participants to decide if they would prefer to do exercises in small groups (four to six members) or as a large group (entire class).

TIPS FOR USING THE DVD

1 Before class time, always view the section of the DVD to be shown in class.

2 When you listen to the DVD, walk through all areas of the room to make sure the volume is set correctly.

3 Have the DVD cued to the right place to start.

4 Make sure all the equipment you need is in class and appropriately connected. This may mean arriving early for class—allowing enough time to preview the DVD.

5 Make sure before your students arrive for class that your video equipment is in good working order.

FINAL WORD

Please note that you will be provided with more material than you need for a 45- to 60-minute group session. We recommend one of three approaches for handling this bounty of teaching resources:

1 Pick and choose. Based on the desires of your class, you may want to emphasize only one area (Bible study, reflection questions, group exercise, experiences with the transforming exercises, etc.) to cover in class—in addition to the DVD presentation.

2 Use two sessions to cover each lesson. Begin each new lesson with a session in which you focus on the DVD lectures and reflection questions, and then allow the class to complete the Bible study and transforming exercises as homework assignments. The second session for each chapter will focus on the group exercise, Bible study, and discussion of each member's experiences with the transformation exercises.

3 Use the materials as part of an extended retreat, again deciding whether to spend one hour or two hours on each chapter.

SESSION ONE:

The Spiritual Disciplines: Door to Liberation

 BEFORE YOU LEAD

■ Quotes and Quips

Joy is the keynote of all the Disciplines. The purpose of the Disciplines is liberation from the stifling slavery to self-interest and fear…. The primary requirement is a longing after God.

Richard J. Foster

God has given us the Disciplines of the spiritual life as a means of receiving his grace. The Disciplines allow us to place ourselves before God so that he can transform us.

Richard J. Foster

The major task of Celebration of Discipline *is to describe this process and to show how the personality can be transformed by the power of the Holy Spirit. It is a practical manual on sanctification.*

Richard J. Foster

■ Key Scripture

If you sow to your own flesh, you will reap corruption from the flesh; but if you sow to the Spirit, you will reap eternal life from the Spirit.

Galatians 6:8

■ Note to Leader

By design, the Leader's Guide provides you with more resources than you can possibly use in a typical 45- to 60-minute group meeting. Here is what we suggest. At the end of each lesson is a one-page outline sheet to help you organize your presentation. Find it first (on CD-ROM or see appendix, p. 29) and use it each week for note taking as you read through the chapter.

Which resources and ideas you use will depend on you and the desires of your group. We assume that each group will want to view the video vignettes on DVD, which feature a presentation by Richard J. Foster and other Renovaré team members. These video vignettes average 22 minutes in length and include a practical or experiential activity for your group. Each vignette closes with worship music that is matched to the particular Spiritual Discipline discussed by Richard.

Following Richard's presentation, the DVD continues for a brief "Soul Talk" session in which Richard Foster and Dallas Willard engage in an unscripted conversation on topics that match the prior vignette. These are "bonus" conversations for which your group is invited to be a fly on the wall and listen in. The average length of these conversations is three to five minutes.

Simply to view the video segment and lead a small group discussion will take approximately 30 minutes—depending, of course, on the length of discussion.

Other featured resources may be seen in the session outline. If your group is to meet for only one session for each Discipline, we suggest that you touch lightly on each topic covered in the outline but give special emphasis (i.e.,

SESSION OUTLINE

I. INTRODUCTION
- ■ Welcome
- ■ Prayer

II. WARM-UP
- ■ Overview/Illustration
- ■ Corresponding Freedom
- ■ Discussion of Homework

III. DVD
- ■ Video Vignette
- ■ Central Truths
- ■ Class Response
- ■ Reflection Questions

IV. BIBLE STUDY
- ■ Leader's Insight
- ■ Group Exercise
- ■ Scripture Meditation

V. EXERCISES FOR...
- ■ Small Group Exercise
- ■ Individual Exercises:
  - • Thoughts • Emotions • Will
  - • Behavior • Social Interactions

VI. SUMMARY
- ■ Richard's Recommendations
- ■ Other Renovaré Resources

time) to only one additional feature (such as the Bible study *or* small group experiential exercise *or* discussion of outside-of-class reading and practice with the particular Discipline).

Note: For groups that wish to complete all the lesson material in more depth, it may be best to spend two meetings on each chapter—one to view the video segment, participate in the group exercise, and discuss both experiences. The second meeting time could then be devoted to the Bible study and discussion of outside-of-class experiences with the practical exercises.

■ Materials

For this session *the leader* will need:
- ■ Leader's Guide
- ■ Bible
- ■ DVD Player, Monitor, Stand, Extension Cord, etc.
- ■ *Celebration of Discipline* DVD
- ■ *Celebration of Discipline* (Chapter One)

For this session *the participant* will need:
- ■ Bible
- ■ Participant's Guide
- ■ Pen or Pencil

INTRODUCTION

■ Welcome

Call the group together and welcome the participants to session one of *Celebration of Discipline*.

Depending on your familiarity with the participants, you may want to introduce yourself—tell the group your name, a little about yourself and your family, and why you are excited to be facilitating this particular class.

■ **Prayer** (See *Prayers From the Heart*, p. 3.)

BE THE GARDENER OF MY SOUL

*SPIRIT OF THE LIVING GOD, be the Gardener of my
Soul. For so long I have been waiting, silent and still—
experiencing a winter of the soul. But now, in the strong
name of Jesus Christ, I dare to ask:*
> *Clear away the dead growth of the past,*
> *Break up the hard clods of custom and routine,*
> *Stir in the rich compost of vision and challenge,*
> *Bury deep in my soul the implanted Word,*
> *Cultivate and water and tend my heart,*
> *Until new life buds and opens and flowers.*
Amen.

WARM-UP

■ **Overview and Illustration**

What function do the Spiritual Disciplines play in producing authentic transformation? And if a Discipline is something you *do*, what is the role of grace in spiritual growth? These are important questions as we launch into this study.

In our key Scripture for this lesson, we find Paul's words to be quite helpful: *"If you sow to your own flesh, you will reap corruption from the flesh; but if you sow to the Spirit, you will reap eternal life from the Spirit"* (Galatians 6:8). Richard Foster uses Paul's analogy and one of his own to help answer our questions about the role of Spiritual Disciplines in producing spiritual growth:

> A farmer is helpless to grow grain; all he can do is provide the right conditions for the growing of grain. He cultivates the ground, he plants the seed, he waters the plants, and then the natural forces of the earth take over, and up comes the grain. This is the way it is with the Spiritual Disciplines—they are a way of sowing to the Spirit. The Disciplines are God's way of getting us into the ground; they put us where he can work within us and transform us. By themselves the Spiritual Disciplines can do nothing; they can only get us to the place where something can be done. They are God's means of grace.
> (*Celebration of Discipline*, p. 7)

From these analogies, the function of the Disciplines comes into focus. They are a means for receiving God's grace, a method for experiencing his love and presence. The Spiritual Disciplines involve human effort, yes, but not earning.

■ Corresponding Freedom

Just as a disciplined athlete is able do what needs to be done when it needs to be done (e.g., throwing a pitch for a strike), a disciplined Christian is able to do what needs to be done when it needs to be done (e.g., showing love to a rebellious teenager).

■ Homework Check-Up

We suggest that the group participants obtain a copy of *Celebration of Discipline* and read the corresponding chapter prior to each session. You may want to suggest this to the group, along with recommending that they read chapters one and two prior to the next meeting.

DVD

■ Video Vignette

In the video segment you will see today, you will have the opportunity to listen to Richard J. Foster as he introduces the Spiritual Disciplines as the pathway to spiritual growth.

During your time in this course, you will see thirteen vignettes—one for each chapter in *Celebration of Discipline*. In each vignette, Richard follows a similar teaching pattern. First, he introduces the topic (after the first session, the topic will always be a specific Spiritual Discipline). Then, through the use of story, humor, and conversation, Richard motivates the audience to practice. Each teaching session concludes with either a practical illustration or an invitation to experience the designated Discipline. Music from RENOVARÉ team members George Skramstad or Jim Stewart marks the end of the video vignette.

But you won't want to turn off the DVD player. After each teaching session, a special bonus feature includes excerpts from a conversation between Richard J. Foster and Dallas Willard. You are invited to stick around and be a fly on the wall for their unscripted dialogue.

Each week there will be approximately 22 minutes of video presentation with an additional three to five minutes of "Soul Talk" conversation between Richard and Dallas Willard. (Note: The "bonus" conversation occurs after the music is finished.)

■ Central Truths (p. 8 in Participant's Guide)

You are provided with a few summary points for the teaching section of each video vignette. Here are the Central Truths for the first video session.

- Galatians 4:19 provides a snapshot of the goal of practicing Spiritual Disciplines. God works with us and invites us into a cooperative relationship with him for the purpose of transformation.
- The Spiritual Disciplines are the primary means whereby we are enabled to bring our individual power packs (our bodies) before God as living sacrifices.
- The process of *indirection* describes the means whereby we participate in something we can do by direct effort (the practice of a Spiritual Discipline) in order to receive resources to do what we could never do by direct effort (loving our enemies).
- The great enemy of successful application of the Spiritual Disciplines is legalism.
- The best place to get started is right where we are.

■ Class Response

Do you have any questions or observations about the video vignettes before we look at the Reflection Questions together?

■ Reflection Questions (p. 9 in Participant's Guide)

Video: Lecture

1 Are you heading toward a clear goal in your spiritual life?

2 What is the role Spiritual Disciplines play in helping you achieve this goal?

③ Richard Foster says that a great enemy of the Spiritual Disciplines is legalism. How is this so?

Book (See *Study Guide for Celebration of Discipline*, p. 12.)

① [Richard says] that "superficiality is the curse of our age." If you tend to agree, list several indicators in [popular] culture that illustrate this.

② Consider carefully Heini Arnold's statement, "We want to make it quite clear that we cannot free and purify our own heart by exerting our own will." How does Arnold's statement compare with your own experience?

③ What [does Richard] mean by "disciplined grace"? What does the concept of "cheap grace" mean? With which of these two types of grace are you most familiar?

BIBLE STUDY

As we consider all this introductory information on the Spiritual Disciplines, let's turn to the Bible for a frame of reference. A short Bible study is found on page 10 in the Participant's Guide and may be used in class. If the discussions have gone overtime, or if you want to spend class time on other activities, you may want to assign the exercise as a homework activity.

Let's get into groups and work through the passage and questions. (The participants may wish to work in small groups of four to six or as a larger group—entire class.)

■ Group Exercise

If time permits, form small groups and allow the participants to complete the Bible study exercise in class. If you are short of time, the Bible study can be completed at home.

Participant's Guide p. 10

■ Leader's Insight

In this passage Paul is offering the insight that it is impossible to confront ingrained habits of sin head-on and win. We cannot control sin, no matter how tight our grip or how white our knuckles. Human willpower is no match for sin. In fact, our will has the same deficiencies as the law: both are able to deal with only surface-level problems.

But we should use our pain. When on the journey of Christian formation we come to the end of ourselves, despairing over our inability to control the process of inner transformation through effort, we are most open to surrender to the indwelling presence of Christ and to the golden revelation that inner righteousness is a gift from God to be graciously received.

■ Scripture Meditation

Please note that the Bible study also includes suggestions for daily Scripture readings (p. 10 in Participant's Guide). Encourage the group participants to spend five to ten minutes with these passages of Scripture each day. As you progress through these sessions, the participants may want to expand this time frame and use these daily passages as part of *lectio divina*. This ancient form of meditation is explained on pages 13, 14 of the Participant's Guide.

TRANSFORMING EXERCISES

Please see pages 11, 12 in the Participant's Guide to observe the suggested *Small Group Exercise* and *Individual Exercises*. The *Small Group Exercise* is designed for use during your session together. The *Individual Exercises* are based on Dallas Willard's five components of the person (i.e., thoughts, emotions, will, behavior, and social interactions) and are constructed for the participants to use as homework activities.

SMALL GROUP

Participant's Guide p. 11

INDIVIDUAL

Participant's Guide p. 12

SUMMARY

■ Review

Celebration of Discipline was written to introduce folks like you and me to the classical Disciplines of the spiritual life. It was a heartfelt call to move us beyond surface-level Christianity and into depths of life with Christ. Perhaps to the surprise of even the author, Richard Foster, it has become a classic.

In listening to Richard's teaching, both on the DVD and in paper-and-ink form, you are witnessing why these ideas are standing the test of time. To use Richard's words, "Our world is hungry for genuinely changed people" (*Celebration of Discipline*, p. 11). *Celebration of Discipline* provides the methodology for making authentic transformation possible. But this does not tell the whole story. *Celebration of Discipline* is not a dry "how to" manual for real change; instead, it is an engaging and articulate storybook that is simultaneously poetic and practical.

So whether you are experiencing *Celebration of Discipline* for the first or the tenth time, the best place to begin is exactly where you are.

■ Richard's Recommendations

Something old: *A Serious Call to a Devout and Holy Life* by William Law, 1686-1761. (New York: Vintage, 2002)

Something new: *The Spirit of the Disciplines* by Dallas Willard. (San Francisco: HarperSanFrancisco, 1991)

■ Other RENOVARÉ Resources

Please visit www.renovare.org for a listing of additional resources for both individual and small group use. For the subsequent lessons we will highlight RENOVARÉ listings that seem most relevant to our topic.

APPENDIX

Use the appendix that follows to facilitate class exercises and homework. The *Bible Study, Small Group Exercise*, and *Individual Exercises* can be found in the Participant's Guide.

Bible Study and Daily Bible Readings
Transforming Exercises (Group and Individual)
Teaching Outline

B I B L E   S T U D Y

Read Colossians 2:20-23.

1   Why is it that determination and effort are never enough to overcome ingrained patterns of sin?

2   Have you ever experienced despair over your own inability to control sin in your life?

3   Why should your despair be an occasion to rejoice?

4   What role do the Spiritual Disciplines play in helping you defeat automatic responses against God and His kingdom rule in your heart?

Daily Scripture Readings (from *Study Guide for Celebration of Discipline*, pp. 11, 12)

Day	Theme	Passage
Sunday	The longing to go deeper	Psalm 42
Monday	The slavery of ingrained habits	Psalm 51
Tuesday	The slavery of ingrained habits	Romans 7:13-25
Wednesday	The bankruptcy of outward righteousness	Philippians 3:1-16
Thursday	Sin in the bodily members	Proverbs 6:16-19
Friday	Sin in the bodily members	Romans 6:5-14
Saturday	The victory of Spiritual Disciplines	Ephesians 6:10-20

SMALL GROUP EXERCISE

Begin Where You Are

As Richard said in the video vignette, the best place to start in practicing Spiritual Disciplines is right where you are. Take a few minutes to consider the twelve Disciplines that will be covered in this course, and provide a ruthlessly honest evaluation of where you are. Simply circle the number that best reflects your current practices, and save this sheet for future reference. After completing the items below, discuss your self-assessment results with the group.

	Never	Rarely	Occasionally	Often	Strong Habit
Inward Disciplines					
Meditation	1	2	3	4	5
Prayer	1	2	3	4	5
Fasting	1	2	3	4	5
Study	1	2	3	4	5
Outward Disciplines					
Simplicity	1	2	3	4	5
Solitude	1	2	3	4	5
Submission	1	2	3	4	5
Service	1	2	3	4	5
Corporate Disciplines					
Confession	1	2	3	4	5
Worship	1	2	3	4	5
Guidance	1	2	3	4	5
Celebration	1	2	3	4	5

INDIVIDUAL EXERCISES

(See *Celebrating the Disciplines: A Journal Workbook to Accompany Celebration of Discipline*, p. 5.)

Thoughts

Invite God to direct your thoughts regarding your expectations for the journey and where it might lead.

Emotions

Reflect with thanksgiving on the presence of the Spirit in your journey through the Disciplines.

Will

Ask God to give you an appropriate orientation of the heart regarding the purposes of your journey.

Behavior

The great enemy of successful application of the Spiritual Disciplines is legalism. Remind yourself that in practicing Spiritual Disciplines, you are simply placing yourself in a better position to receive grace.

Social Interactions

Ask God for the fruit of your practice of Christian Disciplines to be an increased desire to love others with his love.

LECTIO DIVINA

(from "An Introduction to the Practice of Lectio Divina," www.valyermo.com/ld-art.html)

Explanation

Lectio divina is an ancient way of praying the Scriptures, experiencing the Bible as God's living Word. At one time *lectio divina* was a common practice among Christians. It is a slow, contemplative way of allowing the Word and presence of Christ to penetrate to the center of our being and begin a process of transforming us from the inside out.

There are four movements within this method of praying Scripture:

The first movement is called *reading* or *listening*. The practice of *lectio divina* begins with cultivating the ability to listen deeply, to hear "with the ear of our hearts," as St. Benedict describes in the Prologue of his Rule. It is a way of being more sensitive to the still, small voice of God (1 Kings 19:12), the "faint murmuring sound" that is God's Word for us, his voice touching our hearts.

The reading or listening that is the first step in *lectio divina* is very different from the speed-reading you may usually apply to magazines or novels. *Lectio* is reverential listening, listening in a spirit of both silence and awe. In *lectio* we read slowly and attentively, gently listening to hear a word or phrase that is God's communication for us this day.

The second phase of *lectio* is *meditation*. Through listening, we have found a word, passage, or image in the Scripture that speaks to us in a personal way; we must take it in and "ruminate" on it. We ponder it in our hearts. We do so by gently repeating a key word or phrase (or gazing on an image in the passage), allowing it to interact with our thoughts, hopes, memories, and desires. Through this phase, we allow the word from God to become his word for us, a word that touches us at our deepest levels.

The third step in *lectio divina* is *prayer*. Prayer is understood both as dialogue with God, that is, loving conversation with the one who has invited us into his embrace, and as consecration, that is, the priestly offering to God of parts of ourselves that we have not previously believed God wants. Here we allow the word that we have taken in and are pondering to touch and change our deepest selves.

The final step is *rest* in the presence of the one who has used his word as a means of inviting us to accept his transforming embrace. It is the phase called "contemplation," in which there are moments when words are unnecessary. Contemplation is wordless, quiet rest in the presence of the one who loves us.

Meditation

In the practice of *lectio divina* you will choose a text of Scripture that you wish to pray. For this exercise, you are asked to use the text found in the Bible study.

Here is what you do next. After placing yourself in a comfortable position and allowing yourself to become silent, go through the four steps of *lectio divina*.

1 *Read/Listen*. Turn to the text and read it slowly, gently. Savor each portion of the reading, constantly listening for the "still, small voice" of a word or phrase that somehow says, "I am for you today."

2 *Meditate*. Next, take the word or phrase into yourself. Memorize it and slowly repeat it to yourself, allowing it to interact with your inner world of concerns, memories and ideas. Do not be afraid of "distractions." Memories or thoughts are simply parts of yourself. Don't try to chase them away; just return to the word you are pondering.

3 *Converse*. Then speak to God. Whether you use words, ideas, images, or all three is not important. Interact with God as you would with one who you know loves and accepts you. Give to him what you have discovered in yourself during your experience.

4 *Rest*. Finally, you simply rest in God's embrace. Enjoy his presence. And when he invites you to return to your pondering of his word or to your inner dialogue with him, do so. Rejoice in the knowledge that God is with you in both words and silence.

Teaching Outline

BEFORE YOU LEAD: (TIPS FOR FACILITATOR)

I. INTRODUCTION (WELCOME/PRAYER)

II. WARM-UP (OVERVIEW/FREEDOM/DISCUSSION)

III. DVD (VIDEO/TRUTHS/RESPONSE/REFLECTION)

IV. BIBLE STUDY (INSIGHT/EXERCISE/MEDITATION)

V. EXERCISES (GROUP AND INDIVIDUAL)

VI. SUMMARY (RECOMMENDATIONS/RESOURCES)

SESSION TWO:

Meditation

BEFORE YOU LEAD

■ Quotes and Quips

The purpose of meditation is to enable us to hear God more clearly. Meditation is listening, sensing, and heeding the life and light of Christ.

Richard J. Foster

Jesus Christ is alive and here to teach his people himself. His voice is not hard to hear; his vocabulary is not hard to understand. But we must learn how to hear his voice and to obey his word. It is this ability to hear and obey that is the heart and soul of Christian meditation.

Richard J. Foster

Hurry ... is the devil.

Carl Jung

■ Key Scripture

Jesus said to them, "Very truly, I tell you, the Son can do nothing on his own, but only what he sees the Father doing; for whatever the Father does, the Son does likewise."

John 5:19

■ Note to Leader

As you are now aware, the Leader's Guide provides you with more resources than you can use in a typical one-hour group meeting. As with session one, our suggestion is that you locate the one-page outline sheet provided in the appendix to this lesson or on the CD-ROM and use it to organize your presentation.

The resources and ideas you use will depend on you and the desires of your group—which have already come into focus. We assume that most people like overviews and object lessons or stories. So we begin by providing you with some summary quotes, a key Scripture verse, and an overview of what is possible to cover in the lesson. Then, after the welcome and prayer, we give you a brief story or illustration (see Overview and Illustration) to help prepare the class for what is to follow.

We also assume you will be showing the designated DVD segments as part of each class. (Note: It is a good idea to review the video session before each class, as most contain a practical exercise for students to experience in class. You will also want to view the brief conversation Richard Foster has with Dallas Willard at the end of each teaching session to see if you would like to show this "bonus feature" to your group.)

Where you go from there is up to you and your group—but unless you have more than one hour for the class, we don't suggest that you try to do it all.

Some groups may want to focus most of their attention on the Reflection Questions presented in each lesson after the video content is covered. These questions flow from the video content or the text, *Celebration of Discipline*.

SESSION OUTLINE

I. INTRODUCTION
- ■ Welcome
- ■ Prayer

II. WARM-UP
- ■ Overview/Illustration
- ■ Corresponding Freedom
- ■ Discussion of Homework

III. DVD
- ■ Video Vignette
- ■ Central Truths
- ■ Class Response
- ■ Reflection Questions

IV. BIBLE STUDY
- ■ Leader's Insight
- ■ Group Exercise
- ■ Scripture Meditation

V. EXERCISES FOR...
- ■ Small Group Exercise
- ■ Individual Exercises:
  - • Thoughts • Emotions • Will
  - • Behavior • Social Interactions

VI. SUMMARY
- ■ Richard's Recommendations
- ■ Other RENOVARÉ Resources

Other groups may desire to spend the majority of the remaining time together on the Bible study or the transforming exercises. Others may prefer a brief accountability session to discuss all out-of-class activities (reading the corresponding chapters of *Celebration of Discipline* or work with the suggested exercises).

Our desire is to provide a potpourri of resources that you can mix and match to meet the needs of your group.

■ Materials

For this session *the leader* will need:

- ■ Leader's Guide
- ■ Bible
- ■ DVD Player, Monitor, Stand, Extension Cord, etc.
- ■ *Celebration of Discipline* DVD
- ■ *Celebration of Discipline* (Chapter Two)

For this session *the participant* will need:

- ■ Bible
- ■ Participant's Guide
- ■ Pen or Pencil

 ## INTRODUCTION

■ Welcome

Call the group together and welcome the participants to session two of *Celebration of Discipline*. Our Discipline for this time together is meditation.

Depending on the participants' familiarity with one another, you may want to have members (or perhaps just the visitors) introduce themselves individually and state briefly what they hope to get out of this series of meetings.

■ **Prayer** (See *Prayers From the Heart*, p. 79.)

ENTER MY SMALL LIFE

Lord! Give me courage and love to open the door and constrain You to enter, whatever the disguise You come in, even before I fully recognize my guest.

    Come in! Enter my small life!

    Lay Your sacred hands on all the common things and small interests of that life and bless and change them. Transfigure my small resources, make them sacred. And in them

Give me Your very Self.

Amen.

Evelyn Underhill

WARM-UP

■ **Overview and Illustration**

    Is there a biblical basis for meditation? Does Christian meditation differ from other forms? Richard addresses these important questions in *Celebration of Discipline*, as well as in his informative little booklet, *Meditative Prayer* (pp. 4-8). Key excerpts from his answers are provided below.

    The biblical basis for meditation is discovered in the great reality of the speaking, teaching, acting God that lies at the heart of the scriptural witness.

- God brought the universe crashing into existence by the word of his command.
- In the Garden of Eden, Adam and Eve talked with God, *and* God talked with them—they were in communion.
- The Fall resulted in separation from God and a rupture of the communion with him for which we were designed.
- God taught Moses how to hear his voice and obey his words. God spoke to Moses "face to face, as one speaks to a friend" (Exodus 33:11).
- The tabernacle in the wilderness was a symbol of God's desire for communion with his people.
- However, under Moses, God's people rejected immediacy, and under Samuel, they rejected God's theocratic rule: "Give

us a prophet, give us a king, give us a go-between, so we do not have to come into God's presence ourselves."

- In the fullness of time, Jesus came and taught the reality of the kingdom of God and demonstrated what life could be like in that kingdom.
- In his intimate relationship with the Father, Jesus modeled for us the reality of that life of hearing and obeying. "I can do nothing on my own. As I hear, I judge; and my judgment is just, because I seek to do not my own will but the will of him who sent me" (John 5:30).
- During Jesus' commencement address to his disciples, he told them to abide in him, as he abides in the Father. He had told them earlier that he was the good shepherd, and his sheep could learn his voice.
- In the book of Acts, we see the resurrected and reigning Christ, through the Holy Spirit, teaching and guiding his children.

The wonderful news for Christians is that God has never let go of his desire for conversation and communion with his people. Concerning this desire to be with his creation as a gentle shepherd and wise counselor, nothing has changed since the Garden of Eden. In Richard's words, "He is not idle, nor has he developed laryngitis." (*Meditative Prayer*, p. 7)

What distinguishes Christian meditation from other forms is very simple. Christian meditation is the ability to become still, quiet, and focused for the purpose of hearing God's voice more clearly so that we can obey his words.

Okay, but what if I just can't hear?

The story is told about an old man who had become concerned about his wife's hearing (from *Falling for God*, pp. 84, 85). He was convinced that she was not too many days removed from being stone deaf. But he could not get her to admit she had a problem and see a doctor.

One day, he had had enough and decided to prove his point. He entered their living room, where his wife was seated, facing the fireplace. From behind her, he said in a clear voice, "Honey, I love you. Did you hear that?"

No response.

He walked halfway across the room and repeated, "Honey, I said I love you. Do you hear me?"

Nothing.

Finally he walked over, stood in front of her, and shouted, "I love you! Can you hear me now?"

She looked up from her knitting and replied, "Yes, dear, and for the third time, I love you too."

Sometimes when I have been talking to God and have come to believe that he has gone deaf, it's helpful to remember that maybe his ears are just fine and his speech clear. And at those times, if I resolve to devote more time to silent listening and organize my day around being more open to his presence, while I discard competing broadcasts, I'll more often hear him say, "I love you too."

■ Corresponding Freedom

Inward fellowship with God both transforms the inner personality and sends us into our ordinary world with greater perspective and balance.

■ Homework Check-Up

If your group has decided to read the corresponding chapters of *Celebration of Discipline* and participate in the daily Scripture readings or transforming exercises as outside-of-class activities, this is the time to do an accountability check.

DVD

■ Video Vignette

In the first segment of this video presentation, Richard Foster and Glandion Carney provide an introduction to the Discipline of meditation, motivation for practice, and an experiential exercise that focuses on Psalm 95:6, 7.

Each member of your group is encouraged to participate in the meditation and continue in a listening posture through the music that follows.

If your group desires, you can let the DVD continue through a bonus segment called "Soul Talk" and be a fly on the wall for a conversation between Richard and Dallas Willard.

■ Central Truths (p. 16 in Participant's Guide)

You are provided with a few summary points for the teaching section of each video vignette. Here are the Central Truths for the video session about meditation.

- ■ Christian meditation is an open invitation to enter into the wonder-filled "with-God life."
- ■ The biblical word for learning to listen with our hearts is *meditation*.
- ■ The purpose of Christian meditation is to hear God's voice and obey his words.
- ■ Two Hebrew words for meditation are *haga* and *shea*. They imply a process of listening, reflecting, rehearsing, and ruminating.
- ■ There are two classical "books" of meditation, Scripture and nature.
- ■ When Scripture is the focus of our attention, meditation can become like a prism for reflection and openness to insights from God.

■ Class Response

Do you have any questions or observations about the video vignettes before we look at the Reflection Questions together?

■ Reflection Questions (p. 17 in Participant's Guide)

Video: Lecture

1 What experiences have you had with meditation?

2 How do you distinguish Christian meditation from other forms?

3 The first step into meditation involves creating an environment of silence, but learning to listen is also facilitated by learning to practice God's presence throughout the day. What are some things you do that help you live in greater awareness of God presence?

Book (See *Study Guide for Celebration of Discipline*, pp. 21, 22.)

1 What things make your life crowded? Do you think you have a desire to hear the Lord's voice in the midst of the clutter?

2 What threatens you most about meditation?

3 What would you need to do to create a space for meditation in your home?

BIBLE STUDY

Let's turn our attention to the Bible for a frame of reference. A brief Bible study is found on pages 18, 19 in the Participant's Guide and may be used in class or as a homework activity.

◼ Group Exercise

If time permits, form small groups and allow the participants to complete the Bible study exercise in class.

◼ Leader's Insight (from *Falling for God*, pp. 63-65.)

BIBLE STUDY

Participant's Guide p. 18

Consider this passage (Mark 1:21-39) from the perspective of Peter's mother-in-law. Her precious daughter did not marry a doctor, lawyer, or even that tax collector, Matthew. She married a fisherman. Seasonal work. Fish guts to the elbows. Coming home with a stench that would distract a leper. Not the best of jobs, but at least it was a job.

Then along comes a carpenter's son from a town even smaller than Capernaum. Everyone knew nothing good could ever come out of that one-camel town. What's this, is Peter crazy? He's the sole provider for that precious child. He turned in his nets and became unemployed. He gave away his boat—filled with fish! This Jesus is a bad influence. He's got to be put in his place.

But then she gets sick. Real sick. She lies on her bed in a cold sweat. No insurance. No husband. No gainfully employed son-in-law.

Jesus appears in her doorway. Stands over her bed. The troublemaker. The bad influence. She wants to give him a piece of her fevered mind. But look at him. Those eyes. So kind. His touch. Gentle. Real. His touch. It draws her fever away like fatback pulling out a

splinter. Her fever fades, and health comes gushing in and paints her cheeks. Jesus! Maybe he isn't such a bum.

Peter's mother-in-law, with her renewed strength, rises from bed and begins to prepare dinner for Jesus (what a guy) and Peter (maybe not as dumb as he looks).

And then, after the meal, the whole town turns out. Doctors, lawyers, and tax collectors, the sick, the outcasts and demon possessed. Jesus wades into the crowd. What he did for her he does for them all. Fevers stop boiling. Sores disappear. Demons are sent packing. Wow! That Peter is one precocious son-in-law.

But the next morning Peter can't find Jesus—just when he was hoping he would put in a good word with his mother-in-law. Where is he?

Long before the first cock crows, Jesus arises and goes off to a solitary place. He wants to be alone with his Father. He wants to be in his presence, hear his voice so he can better obey that voice.

Hours pass before Peter and his friends catch up with Jesus.

"Let's go back, Jesus. You were right. It has begun. Let's get a tent and hire an organist. It's begun."

But Jesus does not listen. After thousands of years it has indeed begun. But he doesn't go back to the site of the revival. He tells them it's time to move on.

How does he know that? What gives him the fortitude to leave a sure thing and set sail for the uncertain?

The secret—according to Henri Nouwen—is found in the solitary place. That is where Jesus meets with his Father. Alone in an ocean of love. That is where he enjoys his presence and receives direction.

Finding a quiet and lonely place. Ground zero for practicing the presence of God. Ground zero for meditation, availability of the Father. So important. So important that when Jesus dies, the first thing that happens is that the veil in the temple is torn top to bottom. What Jesus discovered, the secret of his ministry, is now available to all. The presence of God. No veils. Just God. Listening and obeying.

At the heart of Christian meditation is taking the time to listen to the voice of God with a settled willingness to obey the Divine whisper.

■ Scripture Meditation

Please note that the Bible study also includes suggestions for daily Scripture readings (page 19 in Participant's Guide). Encourage the group participants to spend five to ten minutes with these passages of Scripture each day. As you progress through these sessions, the participants may want to expand this time frame and use these daily passages as part of *lectio divina*.

TRANSFORMING EXERCISES

Please see pages 20-22 in the Participant's Guide to observe the suggested *Small Group Exercise* and *Individual Exercises*. The *Small Group Exercise* is designed for use during your session together. The Individual Exercises are based on Dallas Willard's five components of the person (i.e., thoughts, emotions, will, behavior, and social interactions) and are constructed for the participants to use as homework activities.

SMALL GROUP

Participant's Guide p. 20

SUMMARY

■ Review

Although each Christian Discipline is simply a different way of being with God and being more open to his transforming presence, meditation is the most logical beginning point for the journey. In meditation we take an off-ramp from the rat race—at least for a few precious minutes—and learn to sink down into the light and life of Jesus. In meditation we learn to become progressively more comfortable with stillness and quiet, and more confident that we may hear the *Kol Yahweh*. Meditation simply means to hear and obey the voice of God.

INDIVIDUAL

Participant's Guide p. 22

■ Richard's Recommendations

Something old: *Some Fruits of Solitude* by William Penn,
1644-1718. (Scottdale, PA: Herald, 2003)

Something new: *Meditative Prayer* by Richard J. Foster.
(Downers Grove, IL: InterVarsity Press,
1983)

■ Other RENOVARÉ Resources

Water & Oil (CD) by Louis Joseph Crescenti. (Orange, CT: Louis
Joseph Crescenti, 1990)

APPENDIX

Use the appendix that follows to facilitate class exercises and
homework. The *Bible Study, Small Group Exercise*, and *Individual
Exercises* can be found in the Participant's Guide.

Bible Study and Daily Bible Readings
Transforming Exercises (Group and Individual)
Teaching Outline

BIBLE STUDY

Read Mark 1:21-39.

① In his marvelous little book *Out of Solitude*, Henri Nouwen said, "Solitude was the secret to Jesus' ministry." What do you think Nouwen meant by that?

② The first thing Mark records in his Gospel after the death of Jesus is the tearing of the veil in the temple. What are the implications of this for you?

③ How does removing yourself from the noise and distractions of the world for a period of time—finding a lonely place, as Jesus did in this passage—relate to the Discipline of meditation?

④ Describe a time when your practice of meditation resulted in increasing your own ability to *hear* and *obey* the voice of God.

Daily Scripture Readings

(from *Study Guide for Celebration of Discipline*, p. 21)

Day	Theme	Passage
Sunday	The glory of meditation	Exodus 24:15-18
Monday	The friendship of meditation	Exodus 33:11
Tuesday	The terror of meditation	Exodus 20:18-19
Wednesday	The object of meditation	Psalm 1:1-3
Thursday	The comfort of meditation	1 Kings 19:9-18
Friday	The insights of meditation	Acts 10:9-20
Saturday	The ecstasy of meditation	2 Corinthians 12:1-4

SMALL GROUP EXERCISE

Preparing to Meditate

While Richard acknowledges that it is impossible to learn to meditate from a book—we learn to meditate by meditating—he does offer some simple suggestions for getting started. (See *Celebration of Discipline: The Path to Spiritual Growth*, pp. 26-28.) These practical steps and a simple exercise in meditation are found below.

Practical Steps

Step One:

Choosing a Time

While the goal is to live life in awareness of God's presence—open and obedient to his voice—it is good in the beginning to make 20- to 30-minute "appointments" with him.

Step Two:

Choosing a Place

Find a place that is quiet and free from interruptions. Make sure that people and phones will not be ringing for attention. It is better to create a designated place in your home.

Step Three:

Choosing a Posture

Even though there is no biblically correct posture for meditation, most people find it helpful to be in a straight-back posture in a comfortable chair with neither arms nor legs crossed. Beds and recliners are death to meditation (but perhaps great for sleeping in the Spirit).

Step Four:

Focus of Attention

The aim is to center your attention—body, emotions, mind, and spirit—upon "the glory of God in the face of Jesus Christ" (2 Cor. 4:6). For some, reading a few verses of Scripture will help with this; others will want to use a picture of Jesus or a special example of religious art; others will want simply to be with Christ in a place free of images and ideas.

A SIMPLE EXERCISE

After completing steps one through three, practice focusing your attention with the following exercise. With your hands on your knees and your palms down, say to God in the rhythm of your slow, deep breathing, "I am letting go of my fear, anger, and self-sufficiency." Then, after five to ten minutes of repeating this prayer, turn your palms up and pray, "I am open and receptive to your voice, your peace, your love, and your direction."

I N D I V I D U A L   E X E R C I S E S

(See *Celebrating the Disciplines: A Journal Workbook to Accompany Celebration of Discipline*, pp. 9, 10.)

Thoughts

Select a Scripture passage on which to meditate in the coming week. If you need a suggestion, you may want to consider the passage cited in our Bible study, or the Lord's Prayer. Write it out on a card you can carry with you, and refer to it often, using spare moments throughout your day to reflect on it. Set aside at least one 20-minute session for focusing on it prayerfully in greater depth.

Emotions

Following a time of Scripture meditation, or simply being still before God and open to his voice, write down the dominant emotion that was present. Ask God to reveal to you what he may wish to communicate through that emotion.

Will

Consecrate one day to seeking opportunities to practice "holy leisure" as a counterpoint to frantic or fragmented activity.

Behavior

Identify a particular place that provides a setting of beauty, and spend 30 minutes there contemplating all the ways in which you can see God's gifts to you in that place. Then try to create a space and a time in your own home for being silent and listening for God's voice each day.

Social Interactions

Sit quietly before God and ask him how you can show his love to those whom you love. Remain in a quiet, listening posture for 20 minutes; then resolve to become an instrument of divine love.

2 2   C E L E B R A T I O N   O F   D I S C I P L I N E

APPENDIX

Teaching Outline

BEFORE YOU LEAD: (TIPS FOR FACILITATOR)

I. INTRODUCTION (WELCOME/PRAYER)

II. WARM-UP (OVERVIEW/FREEDOM/DISCUSSION)

III. DVD (VIDEO/TRUTHS/RESPONSE/REFLECTION)

IV. BIBLE STUDY (INSIGHT/EXERCISE/MEDITATION)

V. EXERCISES (GROUP AND INDIVIDUAL)

VI. SUMMARY (RECOMMENDATIONS/RESOURCES)

Notes

Prayer

BEFORE YOU LEAD

■ Quotes and Quips

A man prayed, and at first he thought that prayer was talking. But he became more and more quiet until in the end he realized that prayer is listening.

Søren Kierkegaard

Prayer—secret, fervent, believing prayer—lies at the root of all personal godliness.

William Carey

True, whole prayer is nothing but love.

St. Augustine

■ Key Scripture

Morning by morning, O Lord, you hear my voice; morning by morning I lay my requests before you and wait in expectation.

Psalm 5:3, NIV

■ Note to Leader

If you have found it useful to use the one-page outline sheet in the appendix or on the CD-ROM in organizing your presentation, you will want to locate it now.

We also assume you have discovered which aspect of these lessons the majority of your class prefers. While we assume that video vignettes and Bible study will be used by most classes, our primary hope is that you will enjoy selecting from the menu of options provided to create a class tailor-made by you to fit the interests of the participants.

And if you've decided it's best to take two weeks to cover a lesson—and do everything suggested—good!

■ Materials

For this session *the leader* will need:

- Leader's Guide
- Bible
- DVD Player, Monitor, Stand, Extension Cord, etc.
- *Celebration of Discipline* DVD
- *Celebration of Discipline* (Chapter 3)

For this session *the participant* will need:

- Bible
- Participant's Guide
- Pen or Pencil

SESSION OUTLINE

I. INTRODUCTION
- Welcome
- Prayer

II. WARM-UP
- Overview/Illustration
- Corresponding Freedom
- Discussion of Homework

III. DVD
- Video Vignette
- Central Truths
- Class Response
- Reflection Questions

IV. BIBLE STUDY
- Leader's Insight
- Group Exercise
- Scripture Meditation

V. EXERCISES FOR...
- Small Group Exercise
- Individual Exercises:
  - Thoughts • Emotions • Will
  - Behavior • Social Interactions

VI. SUMMARY
- Richard's Recommendations
- Other RENOVARÉ Resources

INTRODUCTION

■ Welcome

Call the group together and welcome the participants to session three of *Celebration of Discipline*. Our Discipline for this time together is prayer.

■ Prayer (See *Prayers From the Heart*, p. 62.)

GIVE ME YOURSELF

God, of your goodness give me yourself, for you are enough for me. And only in you do I have everything. Amen.

Lady Julian of Norwich

WARM-UP

■ Overview and Illustration

In his story "Song of the King," Max Lucado describes the adventure of three knights who are all seeking the hand of a fair princess (from *Tell Me the Secrets*, pp. 28-30). The king devises a test. His daughter will marry the brave knight who is able to complete a journey through the dangerous Hemlock Forest.

The first knight is known for his strength, the second for his speed, and the third for alertness—seeing what others miss. To assist the knights, the king will stand on the castle wall three times a day and play a melody on his flute. The music will drift into the forest as a beacon to guide the brave knights. The only other flute of this kind belongs to the king's son.

As it turns out, speed and strength are no match for the dangers of Hemlock Forest. Indeed, the most treacherous aspect of the forest is the fact that Hopenots—small, cunning creatures of the dark woods, who can imitate the sound of the king's flute—populate it.

When, to the surprise of the king, it is the third knight— Cassidon the wise—who completes the crossing, he is asked to describe his success. Cassidon explains that he was able to navigate the dark forest because he chose the right traveling companion—the king's son (the prince), who sat behind him and played the king's song in his ear. "Though a thousand flutes attempted to fool me, I knew your song," he says.

Prayer is a journey in which we learn that the best way to travel through life is by listening for the song of the King. And the best way to keep in step with his music is to choose the right traveling companion, Jesus Christ.

In the Christian Discipline of meditation, we learn to *hear* and *obey*. But in prayer, we experience the more active and interactive aspects of hearing. Prayer goes beyond simple listening. Prayer is also the *conversation* and *communion* we enjoy as we travel *with* God along a pathway that leads to being *consumed* and *transformed* by his love.

■ Corresponding Freedom

Continuous conversation with God produces many benefits; among the greatest of these is the specific joy of learning how to "abide" in his presence.

■ Homework Check-Up

If your group has decided to read the corresponding chapters of *Celebration of Discipline* and participate in the daily Scripture readings or transforming exercises as outside-of-class activities, this is the time to do an accountability check and ask for comments concerning the experiences of any participants who would like to share.

DVD

■ Video Vignette

In the first segment of this video presentation, Richard Foster provides an introduction to the Discipline of prayer as well as motivation for practice and an experiential exercise.

Handwritten notes in left margin:

God's Voice
- Tone
- Quality
- Content
.. Consistent
    thru time

★ No Guarantee that
We've head Correctly

Each group member is encouraged to participate with Richard in this segment by examining his or her own heart for the presence of fears, wounds, or destructive habits. The prayer time concludes with George Skramstad playing "It Is Well With My Soul" as a violin solo.

If your group desires, you can let the DVD continue through a second segment called "Soul Talk" and be a fly on the wall for a conversation between Richard and Dallas Willard. *Book Hearing God S* [handwritten]

■ Central Truths (p. 24 in Participant's Guide)

You are provided with a few summary points for the teaching section of each video vignette. Here are the Central Truths for the video session about prayer.

- The life that is pleasing to God does not come by gritting our teeth, but by falling in love.

- Prayer is not about techniques, definitions, or methods. It is about a hilarious, wonderful, head-over-heels love relationship that God longs to have with us.

- The very heart of God is an open wound of love, desirous of relationship.

- Prayer is the primary way of enjoying the "with-God life."

- There are numerous prayer forms in the Christian tradition, but each is grounded in love. (See appendix to this session, pp. 63-66, or pp. 32-35 in Participant's Guide.)

- Prayer is a way of loving other people.

- Intercessory prayer occurs when we love people enough to desire far more for them than we have the power to give, and this desire leads us to prayer.

■ Class Response

Do you have any questions or observations about the video vignettes before we look at the Reflection Questions together?

■ **Reflection Questions** (p. 25 in Participant's Guide)

Video: Lecture

① What is your reaction to Richard's description of prayer as "a hilarious, wonderful, head-over-heels love relationship with God"?

② How many of the different forms of prayer have you experienced? What is your most and least natural form of prayer? (See appendix to this session, pp. 62-66, or pp. 27-31 in Participant's Guide.)

③ A common misconception about prayer is that it mainly involves asking things from God. How does the teaching by Richard expose this notion as a misunderstanding?

Book (See *Study Guide for Celebration of Discipline*, p. 26)

① What does Richard mean when he says, "To pray is to change"? Have you ever experienced that in your own life?

② What is your response to using the imagination in the work of prayer?

③ What should we do when we don't feel like praying?

BIBLE STUDY

We will now turn our attention to the Bible for a frame of reference. A brief Bible study is found on pages 26, 27 in the Participant's Guide and may be used in class or as a homework assignment.

■ **Group Exercise**

If time permits, form small groups and allow the participants to complete the Bible study exercise in class.

BIBLE STUDY

BIBLE STUDY

Read John 15:7-17.

❶ What are some practical ways in which you "abide" in Christ?

❷ Prior to this passage (see John 15:5), Jesus refers to himself as the vine and his disciples (read also "apprentices" or "friends") as the branches. What is the relationship between abiding in Christ and growing "fruit"?

❸ What is the best way to describe the "fruit" that Christians can bear? (Hint: See Galatians 5:22.)

❹ How is prayer related to abiding in Christ?

❺ What is the difference between being Christ's servant and being his friend?

26   CELEBRATION OF DISCIPLINE

Participant's Guide p. 26

■ Leader's Insight

John presents the last night Jesus spent with his apprentices in chapters 13 through 17 of his Gospel. I like to refer to this section as Jesus' commencement address to his followers. It is replete with object lessons, critical teachings, and prayer.

Notice three of the things Jesus did during this special time: 1) He initiated the first Communion, which became acknowledged by all Christian bodies as the foundational sacrament of the church; 2) He encouraged his followers to remain *in* him as closely as branches remain in a vine; and 3) He prayed to his Father that his disciples would become united with one another, with himself, and with God, just as he and his Father are one.

Think of this from Jesus' perspective. If you had one last evening to spend with your loved ones, what would you say? The most important things, of course! No more time for chitchat; no time for the nonessentials.

Jesus knew that their only prayer of surviving the assaults of the enemy of their souls would be to open their hearts to his presence and power. Their only hope to overcome the world would be to live united.

And right in the center of this commencement address, we find the passage that is the focus of our Bible study, Jesus' special instructions for his friends: "abide in me" (15:7); "bear much fruit" (15:8); "love one another as I have loved you" (15:12); sacrifice as I sacrifice (15:13); and become my friends (15:15).

The great mystery that Paul refers to in Colossians 1:26, 27 is plainly presented by Jesus. The secret of bearing the fruit of Christ's spirit, the secret of loving as Jesus loved is found in the ability to live connected to him, as branches are connected to a vine, his life flowing into our lives.

The secret of Christ-formation is to abide in Christ, and the process of abiding is the process of prayer—activities of conversation, communion, and consuming love.

■ Scripture Meditation

Please note that the Bible Study also includes suggestions for daily Scripture readings (p. 27 in Participant's Guide). Encourage the group participants to spend five to ten minutes with these passages of Scripture each day. As you progress through these sessions, the participants may want to expand this time frame and use these daily passages as part of *lectio divina*.

TRANSFORMING EXERCISES

Please see pp. 28-35 in the Participant's Guide to observe the suggested *Small Group Exercise*, *Individual Exercises*, and "Definitions of Prayer." The *Small Group Exercise* is designed for use during your session together. The *Individual Exercises* are based on Dallas Willard's five components of the person (i.e., thoughts, emotions, will, behavior, and social interactions) and are constructed for the participants to use as homework activities.

SMALL GROUP

Participant's Guide p. 28

INDIVIDUAL

Participant's Guide p. 30

SUMMARY

■ Review

As Richard Foster states in *Celebration of Discipline*, "Prayer catapults us onto the frontier of the spiritual life. Of all the Spiritual Disciplines prayer is the most central because it ushers us into perpetual communion with the Father. Meditation introduces us to the inner life, fasting is an accompanying means, study transforms our minds, but it is the Discipline of prayer that brings us into the deepest and highest work of the human spirit." (p. 33)

■ Richard's Recommendations

Something old: *How to Pray* by Jean-Nicholas Grou,
1730-1803, translated by Joseph Dalby.
(Cambridge: James Clark, 1982)

Something new: *With Christ in the School of Prayer* by
Andrew Murray. (New Kensington, PA:
Whitaker House, 1981)

■ Other RENOVARÉ Resources

Prayer: Finding the Heart's True Home by Richard J. Foster.
(San Francisco: HarperSanFrancisco, 1992)

APPENDIX

Use the appendix that follows to facilitate class exercises and
homework. The *Bible Study, Small Group Exercise*, and *Individual
Exercises* can be found in the Participant's Guide.

Bible Study and Daily Bible Readings
Transforming Exercises (Group and Individual)
Teaching Outline

BIBLE STUDY

Read John 15:7-17.

1   What are some practical ways in which you "abide" in Christ?

2   Prior to this passage (see John 15:5), Jesus refers to himself as the vine and his disciples (read also "apprentices" or "friends") as the branches. What is the relationship between abiding in Christ and growing "fruit"?

3   What is the best way to describe the "fruit" that Christians can bear? (Hint: See Galatians 5:22.)

4   How is prayer related to abiding in Christ?

5   What is the difference between being Christ's servant and being his friend?

Daily Scripture Readings

(from *Study Guide for Celebration of Discipline*, pp. 25, 26)

Day	Theme	Passage
Sunday	The pattern of prayer	Matthew 6:5-15
Monday	The prayer of worship	Psalm 103
Tuesday	The prayer of repentance	Psalm 51
Wednesday	The prayer of thanksgiving	Psalm 150
Thursday	The prayer of guidance	Matthew 26:36-46
Friday	The prayer of faith	James 5:13-18
Saturday	The prayer of command	Mark 9:14-29

S M A L L   G R O U P   E X E R C I S E

Four Simple Steps Into Prayer

In her book *The Healing Light*, Agnes Sanford presents four simple steps into prayer.* Take a few moments to consider a person or situation in your life that needs prayer, but be careful not to start with a complex or long-standing need. Then take a few minutes to walk through these simple steps of prayer.

*See also *Spiritual Classics: Selected Readings for Individuals and Groups on the Twelve Spiritual Disciplines*, p. 38.

Step One

The first step in seeking results by any power is to contact that power. The first step, then, in seeking help from God is to contact God. "Be still, and know that I am God" (Psalm 46:10).

Step Two

The second step is to connect with this life by some prayer such as this: "Heavenly Father, please increase in me at this time your life-giving power."

Step Three

The third step is to believe that this power is coming into use and to accept it by faith. No matter how much we ask for something, it becomes ours only as we accept it and give thanks for it. "Thank you," we can say, "that your life is now coming into me and increasing life in my spirit, my mind, and my body."

Step Four

And the fourth step is to observe the operations of that light and that life. In order to do so, we must decide on some tangible thing that we wish accomplished by that power, so we can know without question whether our experiment succeeded or failed.

Recall your prayer request, and place that person, event, or situation at the feet of Jesus.

INDIVIDUAL EXERCISES

(See *Celebrating the Disciplines: A Journal Workbook to Accompany Celebration of Discipline*, pp. 13, 15.)

Thoughts

Prayer is listening, and prayer is dialogue. To paraphrase Dallas Willard, prayer is talking to God about what we are doing together. For these reasons, we may reasonably consider that we can improve our prayer life by doing things that help us "stay close" to God.

The following are suggested things to do each day that will help us be more mindful of God's presence.
(See *Falling for God*, p. 73.)

Thinking Tips:

Wake up and greet God with a warm "Good Morning," and listen for his response.

Read favorite portions of Scripture as faded love letters—listening for the voice of the author as you read.

Make sure your day planner has at least one appointment with God that is written in indelible ink. Close the door. Offer him an empty chair. Then…shut up, be patient, and lean in.

Emotions

Feeling Tips:

See each person you meet as a new opportunity to show love to the *imago dei* (the image of God buried inside her or him).

Allow hugging your spouse or children to become a sacrament of communicating love to God.

When you turn the light off at night, ask God if he enjoyed your spending the day together, and listen for his response.

Will

Ask God to direct your imagination toward a particular person or context in need of healing, envisioning the restoration that God can bring about. Use this imagery to help guide your prayer.

Behavior

Write John 15:7 and James 4:3 on a card that you can carry with you through the week. Reflect on them often, asking the Spirit to illuminate your understanding of these statements and to open your mind and heart to ways they can enrich your prayer life.

Social Interactions

Frank Laubach said, "I want to learn how to live so that to see someone is to pray for them" (quoted in *Study Guide for Celebration of Discipline*, p. 26). Experiment with that approach to life for one whole day and record what you learn from the experience.

D E F I N I T I O N S   O F   P R A Y E R

(from *Prayer: Finding the Heart's True Home*, as summarized in *Conversations: A Forum for Authentic Transformation* [Spring 2004, 2.1, pp. 30, 31]. Page numbers cited below refer to original text.)

Part One: *Moving Inward: Seeking the Transformation We Need*

Simple Prayer

"In Simple Prayer we bring ourselves before God just as we are, warts and all. Like children before a loving father, we open our hearts and make our requests....We simply and unpretentiously share our concerns and make our petitions." (p. 9)

Prayer of the Forsaken

The prayer we pray when we *sense* that we have been abandoned by God. "The biblical metaphor for these experiences of forsakenness is the desert....Saint John of the Cross named it 'the dark night of the soul.'" (p. 18)

The Prayer of Examen

"[The Prayer of Examen] has two basic aspects, like two sides of a door. The first is the *examen of consciousness* through which we discover how God has been present to us throughout the day and how we have responded to his loving presence. The second aspect is an *examen of conscience* in which we uncover those areas that need cleansing, purifying, and healing." (pp. 27, 28)

The Prayer of Tears

"What is it, this Prayer of Tears? It is being 'cut to the heart' over our distance and offense to the goodness of God (Acts 2:37). It is weeping over our sins and the sins of the world." (p. 37)

The Prayer of Relinquishment

The Prayer of Relinquishment is "a grace-filled releasing of our will and a flowing into the will of the Father. It…moves us from the struggling to the releasing." (p. 47)

Formation Prayer

"The primary purpose of prayer is to bring us into such a life of communion with the Father that, by the power of the Spirit, we are increasingly conformed to the image of the Son. The process of transformation is the sole focus of Formation Prayer." (p. 57)

Covenant Prayer

"Covenant Prayer is a profound interior heart call to a God-intoxicated life. It leads us to the crossroad of personal decision. It guides us through the valley of sacred commitment. It beckons us up the alpine pathway of holy obedience." (p. 67)

> **Part Two:** *Moving Upward: Seeking the Intimacy We Need*

The Prayer of Adoration

"When our reply to God is most direct of all, it is called *adoration*. Adoration is the spontaneous yearning of the heart to worship, honor, magnify, and bless God….We ask for nothing and cherish him." (p. 81)

The Prayer of Rest

"Through the Prayer of Rest God places his children in the eye of the storm. When all around us is chaos and confusion, deep within we know stability and serenity….While a thousand frustrations seek to distract us, we remain focused and attentive. This is the fruit of the Prayer of Rest." (p. 93)

Sacramental Prayer

"Sacramental Prayer is incarnational prayer. [In sacramental prayer] we can be lifted into high, holy reverence by the richness and depth of a well-crafted liturgy…[or] through the warmth and intimacy of spontaneous worship." (p. 105)

Unceasing Prayer

"[Unceasing Prayer is] continual conversations with God." (p. 119)

The Prayer of the Heart

"The Prayer of the Heart is the prayer of intimacy. It is the prayer of love and tenderness of a child to Father God. [Often called 'abba prayer.'] Like the mother hen, who gathers her chicks under her wings, we, through the Prayer of the Heart, allow God to gather us to himself—to hold us, to coddle us, to love us (Luke 13:34)." (p. 131)

Ps 125

Meditative Prayer

"In Meditative Prayer the Bible ceases to be a quotation dictionary and becomes instead 'wonderful words of life' that lead us to *the* Word of life. It differs from the study of Scripture. Whereas the study of Scripture centers on exegesis, the meditation upon Scripture centers on internalizing and personalizing the passage. The written word becomes a living word addressed to us." (p. 146)

Contemplative Prayer

"In its most basic and fundamental expression, Contemplative Prayer is a loving attentiveness to God.…[The goal of contemplative prayer] is union with God." (pp. 158, 159)

Part Three: *Moving Outward: Seeking the Ministry We Need*

Praying the Ordinary

"We pray the ordinary in three ways: first, by turning ordinary experiences of life into prayer; second, by seeing God in the ordinary experiences of life; and third, by praying throughout the ordinary experiences of life." (p. 169)

Petitionary Prayer

"When our asking is for ourselves it is called petition; when it is on

3 4   CELEBRATION OF DISCIPLINE

behalf of others it is called intercession. Asking is at the heart of both experiences." (p. 179)

Intercessory Prayer

"If we truly love people, we will desire for them far more than it is within our power to give them, and this will lead us to prayer. Intercession is a way of loving others." (p. 191)

Healing Prayer

"Healing Prayer is part of the normal Christian life. It should not be elevated above any other ministry in the community of faith, nor should it be undervalued; rather, it should be kept in proper balance. It is simply a normal aspect of what it means to live under the reign of God." (p. 203)

The Prayer of Suffering

In the Prayer of Suffering we leave far behind our needs and wants, even our transformation and union with God. Here we give to God the various difficulties and trials that we face, asking him to use them redemptively. We also voluntarily take into ourselves the griefs and sorrows of others in order to set them free. In our sufferings those who suffer come to see the face of the suffering God." (p. 217)

Authoritative Prayer

"In Authoritative Prayer we are calling forth the will of the Father upon the earth. Here we are not so much speaking *to* God as speaking *for* God. We are not asking God to do something; rather we are using the authority of God to command something done." (p. 229)

Radical Prayer

"Radical Prayer goes to the root, the heart, the center. The word *radical* itself comes from the Latin *radix*, which means root....It dares to believe that things can be different. Its aim is the total transformation of persons, institutions, and societies. *Radical* Prayer, you see, is prophetic." (p. 240)

Teaching Outline

BEFORE YOU LEAD: (TIPS FOR FACILITATOR)

I. INTRODUCTION (WELCOME/PRAYER)

II. WARM-UP (OVERVIEW/FREEDOM/DISCUSSION)

III. DVD (VIDEO/TRUTHS/RESPONSE/REFLECTION)

IV. BIBLE STUDY (INSIGHT/EXERCISE/MEDITATION)

V. EXERCISES (GROUP AND INDIVIDUAL)

VI. SUMMARY (RECOMMENDATIONS/RESOURCES)

Fasting

BEFORE YOU LEAD

Quotes and Quips

Fasting is the voluntary denial of otherwise normal functioning for the sake of intense spiritual activity.

Richard J. Foster

Fasting reveals the things that control us....We are not so much abstaining from food as we are feasting on the word of God. Fasting is feasting!

Richard J. Foster

Some have exalted religious fasting beyond all Scripture and reason; and some others have utterly disregarded it.

John Wesley

Key Scripture

Whenever you fast, do not look dismal, like the hypocrites, for they disfigure their faces so as to show others that they are fasting. Truly I tell you, they have received their reward. But when you fast, put oil on your head and wash your face, so that your fasting may be seen not by others but by your Father who is in secret; and your Father who sees in secret will reward you.

Matthew 6:16-18

■ Note to Leader

If you are using the one-page lesson outlines, you will want to locate that page in the appendix to this lesson or on the CD-ROM now. Please continue to select from the menu of options provided in constructing a lesson tailored to the needs of your group.

■ Materials

For this session *the leader* will need:

- Leader's Guide
- Bible
- DVD Player, Monitor, Stand, Extension Cord, etc.
- *Celebration of Discipline* DVD
- *Celebration of Discipline* (Chapter 4)

For this session *the participant* will need:

- Bible
- Participant's Guide
- Pen or Pencil

SESSION OUTLINE

I. INTRODUCTION
- Welcome
- Prayer

II. WARM-UP
- Overview/Illustration
- Corresponding Freedom
- Discussion of Homework

III. DVD
- Video Vignette
- Central Truths
- Class Response
- Reflection Questions

IV. BIBLE STUDY
- Leader's Insight
- Group Exercise
- Scripture Meditation

V. EXERCISES FOR...
- Small Group Exercise
- Individual Exercises:
  - Thoughts • Emotions • Will
  - Behavior • Social Interactions

VI. SUMMARY
- Richard's Recommendations
- Other RENOVARÉ Resources

INTRODUCTION

■ Welcome

Call the group together and welcome the participants to session four of *Celebration of Discipline*. Our Discipline for this time together is fasting.

■ Prayer (See *Prayers From the Heart*, p. 24.)

A PRAYER OF RELINQUISHMENT

TODAY, O LORD, I yield myself to you.
May your will be my delight today.
May your way have perfect sway in me.
May your love be the pattern of my living.

I surrender to you
my hopes,
my dreams,
my ambitions.
Do with them what you will, when you will, as you will.

I place into your loving care
my family,
my friends,
my future.
Care for them with a care that I can never give.

I release into your hands
my need to control,
my craving for status,
my fear of obscurity.
Eradicate the evil, purify the good, establish your
kingdom on earth.

For Jesus' sake,
Amen.

WARM-UP

■ Overview and Illustration

According to Richard, fasting is a "voluntary denial of otherwise normal functioning for the sake of intense spiritual activity," and, as he states in *Celebration of Discipline*, "more than any other Discipline, fasting reveals the things that control us. This is a wonderful benefit to the true disciple who longs to be transformed into the image of Jesus Christ" (p. 55).

Fasting is not...

- ...about losing weight. This is radical dieting and may be more suggestive of vanity than a desire to be empty of all that is not God.

- ...a way to coerce God into doing something for us He does not wish to do. This idea may suggest both a distorted view of God and a high need for control.

- ...a thinly veiled attempt to draw attention to oneself as a spiritual giant (See Matthew 6:16-18). Such desires may suggest an overly inflated need for the esteem of others, but not a heart's hunger for the presence of God.

Fasting is...

- ...*feasting*—we fast to better concentrate on God and understand what controls us. (*Celebration of Discipline*, p. 55)

To underscore the notion of fasting as feasting, the following exercises are offered and may be incorporated into a future fast.

Use hunger pains as gnawing reminders of the purpose of fasting. When fasting from food, let every sensation of hunger become a reminder that the aim of your self-denial is to be more open to God's instruction and loving presence. Let each sensation of hunger prompt you to sit for a few minutes, resting with God, and pray, "My truest need is for you, God, to be in the center of my being, sustaining every cell in my body with your presence."

Think as you drink. If you are fasting from food, you are most likely drinking water and juices. During your fast, allow each occasion of swallowing a beverage to be a reminder to take a 15-second vacation in which you slowly breathe in and out while praying, "Lord, teach me how to feast on your presence and your word."

■ Corresponding Freedom

Fasting is an opportunity for feasting on God.

■ Homework Check-Up

If your group has decided to read the corresponding chapters of *Celebration of Discipline* and participate in the daily Scripture readings or transforming exercises as outside-of-class activities, this is the time to do an accountability check and ask for comments concerning the experiences of any participants who would like to share.

DVD

■ Video Vignette

In the first segment of this video presentation, Richard Foster provides an introduction to the Discipline of fasting. He is assisted through a discussion with Glandion Carney and Margaret Campbell.

If your group desires, you can let the DVD continue through a second segment called "Soul Talk" and be a fly on the wall for a conversation between Richard and Dallas Willard.

■ Central Truths (pp. 36, 37 in Participant's Guide)

You are provided with a few summary points for the teaching section of each video vignette. Here are the Central Truths for the video section about fasting.

- ■ Fasting is the voluntary denial of an otherwise normal function for the sake of intense spiritual activity.

- ■ In Christian fasting, we are *not* trying to twist God's arm—to manipulate God.

■ Fasting is not to lose weight—not for vanity.

■ In Christian fasting, we are coming alive to the spiritual realm. Fasting makes us more keenly sensitive to the whole of life, so that we do not become obsessed with our consumer mentality.

■ We fast to learn balance in life, to learn the things that control us, to learn how to feast on God.

■ In fasting, we learn that we do not live by bread alone, but by every word that comes from the mouth of God.

■ We learn as much about the Discipline of fasting through our failures as through our successes.

■ Fasting can be used both to remind us of the hungry and to quiet our minds and focus our attention on the need to live dependently upon God.

■ Class Response

Do you have any questions or observations about the video vignettes before we look at the Reflection Questions together?

■ Reflection Questions (p. 37 in Participant's Guide)

Video: Lecture

1 How does Christian fasting differ from a hunger strike and fasting for health?

2 What does it mean to you to learn to feast on God?

3 What have you learned from your failures with fasting? What have you learned from your successes?

Book (See *Study Guide for Celebration of Discipline*, p. 30.)

1 What is the primary purpose of fasting?

2 Define "a normal fast," "a partial fast," and "an absolute fast."

3 What is most difficult about fasting for you?

BIBLE STUDY

If time permits, form small groups and allow the participants to complete the Bible study exercise in class.

■ Group Exercise

We will now turn our attention to the Bible for a frame of reference. A brief Bible study can be found on pages 38, 39 in the Participant's Guide and may be used in class or as a homework assignment.

■ Leader's Insight

In *The Divine Conspiracy*, Dallas Willard offers the following:

> Fasting confirms our utter dependence upon God by finding in him a source of sustenance beyond food. Through it, we learn by experience that God's word to us is a life substance, that it is not food ("bread") alone that gives life, but also the words that proceed from the mouth of God (Matt. 4:4). We learn that we too have meat to eat that the world does not know about (John 4:32-34). Fasting unto our Lord is therefore feasting—feasting on him and on doing his will. ...In fasting we learn to suffer happily as we feast on God. (pp.166, 167)

Dallas' comments help us understand our Bible study passage, Isaiah 58:3-9, wherein God distinguishes between an unacceptable fast and his chosen fast. The contrast in this passage in Isaiah calls to mind the offerings of Cain and Abel. The difference there was not between an offering of plant life (Cain) versus animal life (Abel), but between the two hearts of the givers. Abel's offering of "the firstlings of his flock, their fat portions" was motivated by love and gratitude; it

Participant's Guide p. 38

was an offering of choice. Cain's gift of "the fruit of the ground" was a careless and self-focused (Cain-focused) gift (see Genesis 4:3-5).

The fasting God desires echoes the types of gifts he wants to receive. Both our fasts and our gifts are to begin and end with a centering on God and a heart filled with love. Both are to reflect our joyful acceptance of an utter dependence on God. This stands in marked contrast to fasting or giving that is empty and self-focused. It is not surprising that when our fasting is not feasting, the result is often frustration and anger instead of love.

■ Scripture Meditation

Please note that the Bible Study also includes suggestions for daily Scripture readings (p. 39 in Participant's Guide). Encourage the group participants to spend five to ten minutes with these passages of Scripture each day. As you progress through the sessions, the participants may want to expand the time frame and use these daily passages as part of *lectio divina*.

TRANSFORMING EXERCISES

Please see pages 40, 41 in the Participant's Guide to observe the suggested *Small Group Exercise* and *Individual Exercises*. The *Small Group Exercise* is designed for use during your session together. The *Individual Exercises* are based on Dallas Willard's five components of the person and are constructed for the participants to use as homework activities.

SUMMARY

■ Review

Fasting is perhaps the most disregarded of the Christian Disciplines. As Richard observed in *Celebration of Discipline,* he could not find a single book on this subject published from 1861 to 1954. He hypothesized two explanations for why fasting received so little attention for a period of almost 100 years, continuing until the present: 1) the association of fasting with the excessively ascetic practices of the Middle Ages, and 2) the barrage of consumer propaganda that pushes us toward overindulgence in food.

SMALL GROUP

Participant's Guide p. 40

INDIVIDUAL

Participant's Guide p. 41

Richard reclaims fasting as the Discipline that is most helpful in revealing the things that control us (*Celebration of Discipline*, p. 55) while reminding us that for fasting to be properly practiced, it must be centered on God—God-initiated and God-ordained. The most indelible image from his teaching on fasting is the reminder that as a Christian Discipline, fasting *from* (e.g., food, people, control, the media, etc.) is to be feasting *on* (the presence, power, and love of God). Fasting should reveal what controls us while it provides more of an experiential awareness of who desires communion with us.

◼ Richard's Recommendations

Something old: *Sermon #27, Discourse on the Sermon on the Mount, Matt. 6:16-18* by John Wesley, 1703-1791. http://www.godonthe.net/wesley/jws_027.html

Something new: *God's Chosen Fast* by Arthur Wallis. (Fort Washington, PA: Christian Literature Crusade, 1986)

◼ Other RENOVARÉ Resources

Spiritual Disciplines Index in *The RENOVARÉ Spiritual Formation Bible*, edited by Richard J. Foster. (San Francisco: HarperSanFrancisco, 2005)

APPENDIX

Use the appendix that follows to facilitate class exercises and homework. The *Bible Study, Small Group Exercise*, and *Individual Exercises* can be found in the Participant's Guide.

Bible Study and Daily Bible Readings
Transforming Exercises (Group and Individual)
Teaching Outline

BIBLE STUDY

Read Isaiah 58:3-9.

1 How would you describe the Lord's chosen fast?

2 How did the people's view of fasting differ from God's?

3 Are there any religious activities in which you feel as if you are just going through the motions: Reading the Bible? Attending church? Communion services? Fasting?

4 What attitudes are needed for these Disciplines to be pleasing to God?

5 What is the connection between Spiritual Disciplines (like fasting) and love for others?

Daily Scripture Readings

(from *Study Guide for Celebration of Discipline*, p. 30)

Day	Theme	Passage
Sunday	The example of Christ	Luke 4:1-13
Monday	God's chosen fast	Isaiah 58:1-7
Tuesday	A partial fast	Daniel 10:1-14
Wednesday	A normal fast	Nehemiah 1:4-11
Thursday	An absolute fast	Esther 4:12-17
Friday	The inauguration of the gentile mission	Acts 13:1-3
Saturday	The appointment of elders in the churches	Acts 14:19-23

SMALL GROUP EXERCISE

The Practice of Fasting

(See *Celebrating the Disciplines: A Journal Workbook to Accompany Celebration of Discipline*, p. 19.)

If you have never fasted before, you might want to consider experimenting with a brief fast this week. If you are experienced with the Discipline of fasting, you might reflect on a theme or focus suggested in *Celebration of Discipline* (see below). After reviewing the following three ideas, discuss as a group your specific plan for experiencing a fast this week. (Note: You may want to adopt one of the suggestions from the Individual Exercises that follow.)

Ideas for Practicing Fasting

- If you have not fasted before, plan a fast of two or more meals' duration—breakfast to breakfast, lunch to lunch, and so on— when you will consume only fruit juice and water. Seek a "gentle receptiveness to divine breathings" during your fast. Afterward, monitor your physical, mental, emotional, and spiritual responses to the fast.

- If you have fasted before, plan a fast of whatever duration is right for you this week. Perhaps this would be an appropriate time to reflect and pray about your journey into the Spiritual Disciplines in the months ahead.

- Fast from something that does not involve food—for example, the entertainment media, passing judgment on yourself or others, people (to experience solitude), or impulsive speech.

40   CELEBRATION OF DISCIPLINE

INDIVIDUAL EXERCISES

The key idea with fasting is the voluntary denial of an otherwise normal activity or function for the sake of spiritual growth. While Scripture deals with fasting in regard to food, Richard has taken this core principle and applied it to other aspects of contemporary culture.* Consider a fast corresponding to each of the components of a person.

Thoughts

Our thinking is saturated by mass media. Declare one day next week media-free and avoid television, the Internet, radio, magazines, and newspapers. At the end of the day, take notes on what you learned.

Emotions

For one day, agree not to entertain anger or criticism. At the initial onset of emotion (or cognition), shift the focus of your attention to some other event or activity. Consider the outward beauty of a flower or the potential inward beauty of the person with whom you are angry.

Will

As an act of the will, take a day and fast from the telephone. If this seems impossible, then consider a partial fast and commit to ignore the telephone during meal times and for a set period of time that you will spend with your family or a friend.

Behavior

For the entire week, make a commitment that you will make no consumer purchases unless utility demands it (e.g., purchasing food when the cabinets are bare, or paying the electricity bill)

Social Interactions

Learn to fast from people. For at least one four-hour block (during your waking hours) enjoy silence and solitude.

*See both *Study Guide for Celebration of Discipline*, pp. 28-30, and *Freedom of Simplicity*, pp. 138, 139.

Teaching Outline

BEFORE YOU LEAD: (TIPS FOR FACILITATOR)

I. INTRODUCTION (WELCOME/PRAYER)

II. WARM-UP (OVERVIEW/FREEDOM/DISCUSSION)

III. DVD (VIDEO/TRUTHS/RESPONSE/REFLECTION)

IV. BIBLE STUDY (INSIGHT/EXERCISE/MEDITATION)

V. EXERCISES (GROUP AND INDIVIDUAL)

VI. SUMMARY (RECOMMENDATIONS/RESOURCES)

SESSION FIVE:

Study

BEFORE YOU LEAD

■ Quotes and Quips

Do not be conformed to this world, but be transformed by the renewing of your minds, so that you may discern what is the will of God—what is good and acceptable and perfect.

St. Paul (Romans 12:2)

The purpose of the Spiritual Disciplines is the total transformation of the person. They aim at replacing old destructive habits of thought with new life-giving habits. Nowhere is this purpose more clearly seen than in the Discipline of study.

Richard J. Foster

The mind will always take on an order that conforms to the order of whatever it concentrates upon.

Richard J. Foster

■ Key Scripture

Then Jesus said to the Jews who had believed in him, "If you continue in my word, you are truly my disciples; and you will know the truth, and the truth will make you free."

John 8:31, 32

■ Note to Leader

If you are using the one-page lesson outlines, you will want to locate that page in the appendix to this lesson or on the CD-ROM now. Please continue to select from the menu of options provided in constructing a lesson tailored to the needs of your group.

■ Materials

For this session *the leader* will need:

- Leader's Guide
- Bible
- DVD Player, Monitor, Stand, Extension Cord, etc.
- *Celebration of Discipline* DVD
- *Celebration of Discipline* (Chapter 5)

For this session *the participant* will need:

- Bible
- Participant's Guide
- Pen or Pencil

SESSION OUTLINE

I. INTRODUCTION
- Welcome
- Prayer

II. WARM-UP
- Overview/Illustration
- Corresponding Freedom
- Discussion of Homework

III. DVD
- Video Vignette
- Central Truths
- Class Response
- Reflection Questions

IV. BIBLE STUDY
- Leader's Insight
- Group Exercise
- Scripture Meditation

V. EXERCISES FOR...
- Small Group Exercise
- Individual Exercises:
  - Thoughts • Emotions • Will
  - Behavior • Social Interactions

VI. SUMMARY
- Richard's Recommendations
- Other RENOVARÉ Resources

INTRODUCTION

■ Welcome

Call the group together and welcome the participants to session five of *Celebration of Discipline*. Our Discipline for this time together is study. Encourage the group to reflect on the words and images of this classic prayer as you pray it aloud.

■ Prayer (from *The Book of Common Prayer*, p. 364.)

THE LORD'S PRAYER

Our Father, who art in heaven,
    hallowed be thy Name,
    thy kingdom come,
    thy will be done,
        on earth as it is in heaven.
Give us this day our daily bread.
And forgive us our trespasses,
    as we forgive those
        who trespass against us.
And lead us not into temptation,
    but deliver us from evil.
    For thine is the kingdom,
        and the power, and the glory,
        for ever and ever. Amen.

WARM-UP

■ Overview and Illustration

Dallas Willard observes, "The human spirit is an inescapable, fundamental aspect of every human being; and it takes on whichever character it has from the experiences and the choices that we have lived through or made in the past" (*Renovation of the Heart: Putting On the Character of Christ*, p. 13). To put this another way, to live is to be formed. We are formed when we hear a sermon or read

Scripture, yes, but we are also being formed by the commercials we watch on television, by our work environments, conversations, and the songs we listen to while driving to work.

Because the mind can be so easily "deformed" through *accidental* study, putting purposeful study into our daily routines is vitally important. According to Foster, "Study is a specific kind of experience in which through careful attention to reality the mind is enabled to move in a certain direction....The mind will always take on an order conforming to the order upon which it concentrates." (*Celebration of Discipline,* p. 63)

While four specific steps of study—repetition, concentration, comprehension, and reflection—will be presented in our Bible study, it may be more helpful to point out that we study a book the same way we study a person—or even nature.

For a long time I have been fascinated by the fact that teaching people how to get the most out of a book involves the same pattern as teaching a person how to be a good counselor. You really can read a person like a book.

Getting to Know a Person—or a Book

A well-trained counselor will be able to sit with a person and orchestrate three levels of interaction.

First: Listen for understanding. A good counselor is able to be quiet, suspend judgment, and simply listen to another person—for hours if necessary. The first goal in counseling is the same as that of reading: to understand what is being said. To reach this goal takes time, intentionality, and patience. In Richard's four steps, this corresponds to "repetition" and "concentration."

Second: Listen for insights. An even better counselor is able to add insight to understanding. What does the communication really mean? Are there repeated patterns in the person's words, or life, that are very important? Whether one is listening to a person or reading a book, it is important to know what all the words really mean. This corresponds to "comprehension" in Richard's model.

Third: Listen for evaluation. Finally, a seasoned counselor is able to add a third phase to his or her work. To understanding is added insight, and to insight, evaluation and action. What needs to be done? What changes need to be made? A thorough reading of a person or a book needs to take us to evaluation, action, and, ultimately, change. This third movement in learning how to understand people seems roughly analogous to Richard's use of "reflection," particularly if it leads to change or action.

Understanding, Insight, and *Evaluation/Action* are not only the three classic movements of counseling, but they are also what Mortimer J. Adler refers to as the three intrinsic rules that govern study (see Adler's *How to Read a Book,* referenced in *Celebration of Discipline,* pp. 67, 68).

Getting to Know God

Carved over the door to the main library at Harvard University is the inscription "The truth shall make you free." This is fascinating for at least two reasons. First is the use of a Bible verse (the quote is taken from John 8:32) in such a prominent location at Harvard. Second is what's missing. This carved fraction of a verse is missing its very important context:

"Then Jesus said to the Jews who had believed in him, 'If you continue in my word, you are truly my disciples; and you will know the truth, and the truth will make you free'" (John 8:31, 32).

Freedom does not come by walking into the library or through the study of thousands of books. It is continuing (read also, "abiding") in Christ's words that will bring freedom. It is through studying his words—taking the time to understand, gain insights, and be changed by profound new truths—that we are made free.

According to Foster, "Study is a specific kind of experience in which through careful attention to reality the mind is enabled to move in a certain direction" (*Celebration of Discipline,* p. 63). Abiding in the words of Christ is the highest and most impactive form of study and the source of freedom and transformation.

■ Corresponding Freedom

Study enables us to take on the mind of Christ.

■ Homework Check-Up

If your group has decided to read the corresponding chapters of *Celebration of Discipline* and participate in the daily Scripture readings or transforming exercises as outside-of-class activities, this is the time to do an accountability check and ask for comments concerning the experiences of any participants who would like to share.

DVD

◼ Video Vignette

In the first segment of this video presentation, Richard Foster provides an introduction to the Discipline of study. He is assisted through a discussion with Glandion Carney and Margaret Campbell.

If your group desires, you can let the DVD continue through a second segment called "Soul Talk" and be a fly on the wall for a conversation between Richard and Dallas Willard.

◼ Central Truths (pp. 42, 43 in Participant's Guide)

You are provided with a few summary points for the teaching section of each video vignette. Here are the Central Truths for the video session about study.

- ◼ Study is the Spiritual Discipline in which the mind takes on an order conforming to the order of whatever it is concentrating on.

- ◼ This process of conforming can happen even without a deliberate attempt to do so (Richard's example of listening to music from the musical *Oklahoma*).

- ◼ In the Christian Discipline of study we are coming to understand who God is, what God is like, and how God works with his children.

- ◼ John, in his Gospel, defines eternal life as the knowledge of God.

- ◼ To think rightly about God is, in an important sense, to have everything right. To think wrongly about God is to have everything wrong.

- ◼ Because the Discipline of study is so important for transformation, it should be part of normal church life for all Christians.

■ The function of study is not to amass knowledge but to come to know a life, the life of God and the life of Jesus Christ.

■ It is the Spirit of God that illuminates Scripture for us and guides us into all truth.

■ The four steps of study are these:
1. *Repetition*—repeated exposure.
2. *Concentration*—focus, intensity, and intentionality.
3. *Comprehension*—the "aha" of deep understanding.
4. *Reflection*—considering the significance of what we are studying.

■ We study not only the Bible—the supreme book—but also nature, human experience, and the great devotional masters.

■ By our study of the devotional masters, the saints can become our counselors.

■ Class Response

Do you have any questions or observations about the video vignettes before we look at the Reflection Questions together?

■ Reflection Questions (p. 43 in Participant's Guide)

Video: Lecture

1 Have you ever had an experience with "accidental" study (similar to Richard's experience with the musical *Oklahoma*)? How do you minimize the accidental study of "deforming" material?

2 What are some ways you can use the Discipline of study to think rightly about God?

3 Outline a plan for using study to help you take on the mind of Christ.

Book (See *Study Guide for Celebration of Discipline*, p. 34.)

1 Why does study more fully bring about the purpose of the Spiritual Disciplines, which is the transformation of the individual? In other words, what does study do that the other Disciplines do not?

2 The four steps into study that [Richard] gives are repetition, concentration, comprehension, and reflection. Which of these four steps do you feel is the most important in bringing about the goal of the transformation of the individual?

3 Outside of the Bible, what book has had the most profound impact upon your own life? Why?

BIBLE STUDY

If time permits, form small groups and allow the participants to complete the Bible study exercise in class.

■ Group Exercise

Again we will turn our attention to the Bible for a frame of reference. A brief Bible study can be found on pages 44, 45 in the Participant's Guide and may be used in class or as a homework assignment.

■ Leader's Insight

In this session the Bible study involves a direct application of the *Four Steps of Study* (see pp. 64-66 of *Celebration of Discipline*) to a passage of Scripture, John 10:1-14, 27, 28. These steps are as follows.

BIBLE STUDY

Read John 10:1-14, 27, 28.

1 *Repetition.* Slowly read through the biblical text two or three times. What did you observe in the text during your second or third readings that you missed the first time?

2 *Concentration.* Focus in on verses 10:4, 10, 27, and 28. Read this cluster of verses three or four times. As best you can, allow all of your attention to focus on these words. Which images or ideas in these verses do you want to understand at the deepest possible level?

3 *Comprehension.* In Jesus' setting, shepherds led sheep and did not force them to follow—unlike cattle drovers. The sheep trusted the shepherd and came to know his voice. In the four verses on which you have been concentrating, it seems that Jesus desires for his followers to be able to recognize his voice and to follow him to places where life is abundant (overflowing) and eternal. Please take a few moments to focus on the truth of this profound offer.

4 *Reflection.* What is the significance of this passage for your life? How does the truth in this passage make you want to live life differently? What is your plan for doing so—beginning today?

44   CELEBRATION OF DISCIPLINE

Participant's Guide p. 44

1. *Repetition.*   Repetition involves regularly channeling the mind in a specific direction, thus ingraining habits of thought. (p. 64)

2. *Concentration.*   Concentration centers the mind. It focuses the attention on what is being studied. (p. 65)

3. *Comprehension.* Comprehension adds understanding to repetition and focus. (p. 65)

4. *Reflection.* Reflection defines the significance of what we are studying. (p. 66)

For the purpose of this Bible study, *repetition* is accomplished through taking the time to allow each member of the group to read through the passage two or three times. You may want to do this through allowing quiet time for silent reading, or your group may prefer to listen to a designated reader.

In applying the step of *concentration*, it is suggested that key verses (John 10:4, 10, 27, 28) be reread and given focused attention—with openness to deeper understanding of key images and ideas.

Finally, *comprehension* and *reflection* are encouraged as the student of this passage considers what it means to hear the voice of the good shepherd and to follow along the path to abundant and eternal life.

■ Scripture Meditation

Please note that the Bible Study also includes suggestions for daily Scripture readings (p. 45 in Participant's Guide). Encourage the group participants to spend five to ten minutes with these passages of Scripture each day. As you progress through these sessions, the participants may want to expand this time frame and use these daily passages as part of *lectio divina*.

TRANSFORMING EXERCISES

Please see pages 46-49 in the Participant's Guide to observe the suggested *Small Group Exercise* and *Individual Exercises*. The *Small Group Exercise* is typically designed for use during your session together—although this will require additional practice at home. The *Individual Exercises* are based on Dallas Willard's five components of the person and are constructed for the participants to use as homework activities.

SMALL GROUP

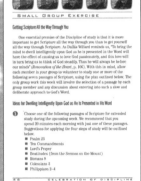

Participant's Guide p. 46

INDIVIDUAL

Participant's Guide p. 48

SUMMARY

■ Review

As Paul references in Romans 12:2, we are transformed through the renewing of our minds. Richard Foster echoes this when he says, "The mind is renewed by applying it to those things that will transform it" (*Celebration of Discipline*, p. 62). While the purpose of each Spiritual Discipline is to replace old, destructive habits with new, life-giving patterns, the Discipline of study brings this aim into the clearest focus.

In this session we present practical applications of the four steps of study—*repetition*, *concentration*, *comprehension*, and *reflection*—while offering two important reminders. First, formation also happens "accidentally," that is, passively. Since to live is to be formed, it is important to be very deliberate about all activities of the mind. Second, in addition to Scripture and the writings of devotional masters, it is important that we also study nature, beauty, and humanity.

He that studies only men will get the body of knowledge without the soul; and he that studies only books, the soul without the body. He that to what he sees, adds observation, and to what he reads, reflection, is in the right road to knowledge, provided that in scrutinizing the hearts of others, he neglects not his own.

—Caleb Colton
(quoted in *Celebration of Discipline*, p. 62)

■ Richard's Recommendations

Something old: *Pensees* by Blaise Paschal, 1623-1662.
                              (New York: Penguin, 1995)

Something new: *How to Read a Book* by Mortimer J. Adler.
                              (New York: Simon & Schuster, 1940)

■ Other RENOVARÉ Resources

The RENOVARÉ Spiritual Formation Bible, edited by Richard J. Foster. (San Francisco: HarperSanFrancisco, 2005)

APPENDIX

Use the appendix that follows to facilitate class exercises and homework. The *Bible Study, Small Group Exercise*, and *Individual Exercises* can be found in the Participant's Guide.

Bible Study and Daily Bible Readings
Transforming Exercises (Group and Individual)
Teaching Outline

BIBLE STUDY

Read John 10:1-14, 27, 28.

① *Repetition.* Slowly read through the biblical text two or three times. What did you observe in the text during your second or third readings that you missed the first time?

② *Concentration.* Focus in on verses 10:4, 10, 27, and 28. Read this cluster of verses three or four times. As best you can, allow all of your attention to focus on these words. Which images or ideas in these verses do you want to understand at the deepest possible level?

③ *Comprehension.* In Jesus' setting, shepherds led sheep and did not force them to follow—unlike cattle drovers. The sheep trusted the shepherd and came to know his voice. In the four verses on which you have been concentrating, it seems that Jesus desires for his followers to be able to recognize his voice and to follow him to places where life is abundant (overflowing) and eternal. Please take a few moments to focus on the truth of this profound offer.

④ *Reflection.* What is the significance of this passage for your life? How does the truth in this passage make you want to live life differently? What is your plan for doing so—beginning today?

Daily Scripture Readings

(from *Study Guide for Celebration of Discipline*, pp. 33, 34)

Day	Theme	Passage
Sunday	The call to study	Proverbs 1:1-9, 23:12, 23
Monday	The source of truth	James 1:5, Hebrews 4:11-13, 2 Timothy 3:16-17
Tuesday	What to study	Philippians 4:8-9, Colossians 3:1-17
Wednesday	The value of study	Luke 10:38-42
Thursday	Active study	Ezra 7:10, James 1:19-25
Friday	Study in the evangelistic enterprise	Acts 17:1-3, 17:10-12, 19:8-10
Saturday	The study of a nonverbal book	Proverbs 24:30-34

S M A L L   G R O U P   E X E R C I S E

Getting Scripture All the Way Through You

One essential premise of the Discipline of study is that it is more important to get Scripture all the way through you than to get yourself all the way through Scripture. As Dallas Willard reminds us, "To bring the mind to dwell intelligently upon God as he is presented in the Word will have the effect of causing us to love God passionately, and this love will in turn bring us to think of God steadily. Thus he will always be before our minds" (*Renovation of the Heart*, p. 106). With this in mind, allow each member in your group to volunteer to study one or more of the following seven passages of Scripture, using the plan outlined below. The only group work this week will involve the selection of a passage by each group member and any discussion about entering into such a slow and deliberate approach to God's Word.

Ideas for Dwelling Intelligently Upon God as He Is Presented in His Word

❶ Choose one of the following passages of Scripture for extended study during the upcoming week. We recommend that you spend 20 minutes each morning with just one of these passages. Suggestions for applying the four steps of study will be outlined below.
   - Psalm 23
   - Ten Commandments
   - Lord's Prayer
   - Beatitudes (from the Sermon on the Mount)
   - Romans 8
   - Colossians 3
   - Philippians 2–4

② *Repetition.* For your first study session, read and reread the one passage you will be working with this week. Be sensitive to any key verses, images, or even a single word you wish to explore more fully.

③ *Concentration.* For your second study session, apply *lectio divina* as a method for concentrating on your passage. (Note: if you chose a passage of Scripture that is more than ten or twelve verses in length, you may wish to concentrate on just part of the overall passage.)

④ *Comprehension.* Spend two or three days studying your passage with the help of a study Bible and biblical commentaries.

⑤ *Reflection.* Spend your remaining study sessions asking God how he would like to apply insights from your study passage to your life. Return to the group next week prepared to share what you learned from your study sessions with God.

INDIVIDUAL EXERCISES

(See *Celebrating the Disciplines: A Journal Workbook to Accompany Celebration of Discipline,* pp. 23. 24.)

Thoughts

Choose a brief selection from a book and practice the four steps of repetition, concentration, comprehension, and reflection. Ask yourself, "Do I read to be changed by the truth or to avoid doing the truth?"

Emotions

Choose one member of your family (spouse or child) and take him or her out for a breakfast or lunch. While spending time with this loved one, listen, really listen, to whatever he wants to talk about. Listen for the content of what she is saying, and listen for any expression of emotion. Do not offer advice. Simply listen for the purpose of understanding her better. At the end of the time together, let him know you understood what was said and that to some extent you felt (empathized) with any expression of emotion.

Will

As Richard Foster points out, we are not only formed through purposeful study, but also deformed through accidental study—passive exposure to television, billboards, radio, music, conversations, etc. For one week, keep a log sheet by each television in your home, and monitor each program or partial program that any member of your family watches. Then total the number of hours spent watching, and note the names of shows watched. Have a family discussion about the pros and cons of these formation activities.

Behavior

Schedule an interlude in an appropriate location in order to concentrate on studying the book of nature. In what sense does study of nature differ for you from meditation on nature?

Social Interactions

Spend several study sessions with Jesus' commencement address to his friends (John 13–17). As you read these important words, consider what is said about Jesus' relationship with his Father and with his friends. Be challenged to experience more friendship with God and to be more loving in all social relationships.

Teaching Outline

BEFORE YOU LEAD: (TIPS FOR FACILITATOR)

I. INTRODUCTION (WELCOME/PRAYER)

II. WARM-UP (OVERVIEW/FREEDOM/DISCUSSION)

III. DVD (VIDEO/TRUTHS/RESPONSE/REFLECTION)

IV. BIBLE STUDY (INSIGHT/EXERCISE/MEDITATION)

V. EXERCISES (GROUP AND INDIVIDUAL)

VI. SUMMARY (RECOMMENDATIONS/RESOURCES)

Simplicity

BEFORE YOU LEAD

Quotes and Quips

The central point for the Discipline of simplicity is to seek the kingdom of God and the righteousness of his kingdom first, and then everything necessary will come in its proper order.

Richard J. Foster

The inward reality of simplicity involves a life of joyful unconcern for possessions.

Richard J. Foster

Because we lack a divine Center, our need for security has led us to an insane attachment to things.

Richard J. Foster

Key Scripture

Strive first for the kingdom of God and his righteousness, and all these things will be given to you as well.

Matthew 6:33

■ Note to Leader

If you are using the one-page lesson outlines, you will want to locate that page in the appendix to this lesson or on the CD-ROM now. Please continue to select from the menu of options provided in constructing a lesson tailored to the needs of your group.

■ Materials

For this session *the leader* will need:

- Leader's Guide
- Bible
- DVD Player, Monitor, Stand, Extension Cord, etc.
- *Celebration of Discipline* DVD
- *Celebration of Discipline* (Chapter 6)

For this session *the participant* will need:

- Bible
- Participant's Guide
- Pen or Pencil

SESSION OUTLINE

I. INTRODUCTION
- Welcome
- Prayer

II. WARM-UP
- Overview/Illustration
- Corresponding Freedom
- Discussion of Homework

III. DVD
- Video Vignette
- Central Truths
- Class Response
- Reflection Questions

IV. BIBLE STUDY
- Leader's Insight
- Group Exercise
- Scripture Meditation

V. EXERCISES FOR...
- Small Group Exercise
- Individual Exercises:
  - Thoughts • Emotions • Will
  - Behavior • Social Interactions

VI. SUMMARY
- Richard's Recommendations
- Other RENOVARÉ Resources

INTRODUCTION

■ Welcome

Call the group together and welcome the participants to session six of *Celebration of Discipline*. Our Discipline for this time together is simplicity.

■ Prayer (See *Prayers From the Heart*, p. 5.)

GIVE US THAT SUBLIME SIMPLICITY

Suffer us, O Father, to come to Thee.
Lay Thy hands on us and bless us.
Take away from us forever our own spirit and replace it
by the instinct of Thy divine grace.
Take away from us our own will and leave us
only the desire of doing Thy will.
Give us that beautiful, that lovable, that
sublime simplicity which is the first and
greatest of Thy gifts.
Amen.

J.N. Grou

WARM-UP

■ Overview and Illustration

In the movie *City Slickers*, Mitch Robbins (Billy Crystal) is an urbanite standing on the edge of a midlife crisis. In hopes of finding a cure, Mitch and two friends decide to go on a two-week cattle drive from New Mexico to Colorado. Since the three city slickers know nothing about riding, roping, and wrangling, they are taken under the firm guidance of Curly (Jack Palance), a leathery-tough trail hand.

In a poignant scene Curly tells Mitch something like this: "You city folks are all alike. You spend a lifetime getting tied up in knots

and think that spending a couple of weeks out here will straighten you out. But you won't be fixed that way. What's important is that you find the *one thing*."

When Mitch realizes Curly hasn't told him what that one thing is, he calls after him. But Curly doesn't provide the answer. It's up to Mitch to find his own *one thing*.

In this chapter, Richard Foster plays a more accommodating Curly. He suggests that the life-healing benefits of the Discipline of simplicity will untie our knots, and he even unpacks the secret. Simplicity is achieved by doing *one thing*. The *one thing* is this: Seek first the kingdom of God. "Everything hinges upon maintaining the 'first' thing as first. Nothing must come before the kingdom of God, including the desire for a simple life-style" (*Celebration of Discipline*, p. 86). Finding the freedom of simplicity begins and ends with seeking first the kingdom of God.

If time permits, you may want to share the following story with the class. It's about how one little boy taught me to discover the kingdom of God (from *Falling for God*, pp. 39-41).

Dancin' Boy

When time and money permit, my family likes to plan vacations by allowing each person to pick the place he or she most wants to visit, and then connecting the dots. Prince Edward Island made the itinerary because one of my two daughters watched *Anne of Green Gables* until the pictures fell off the videotape. Naturally, she would want to see the place that inspired the author.

We were staying at a bed-and-breakfast that was part of a working farm—with pigs to be slopped, cows to be milked, and sheep hooked directly to a loom. The farm was a few hundred feet behind one of the only three colleges of piping in the world. I assumed it was a school that taught plumbers how to connect pipe and wear their pants, but I was wrong.

Our first morning there, I awoke to the sound of a cat being strangled. The noise went on for what seemed like hours. I was just about to get up and go help the cat fight back when my wife said, "Don't you just love bagpipes?"

About as much as I love a rousing polka or an ice-cream headache, I thought. Then it dawned on me. We were staying within earshot of a place where they train wannabe bagpipers. No wonder they only allow three of these colleges in the world. Probably tightly controlled by the United Nations.

That evening, however, we found ourselves sitting in an audience of a Celtic arts festival. Fortunately, the teachers at the college put it on, and it was outstanding. Two hours of Celtic folk songs, river dances, drums, and fiddling made the occasional cat strangling tolerable.

At one point, while a three-piece band was at full throttle, the drummer broke rank and stepped to center stage. He put on the most amazing display of percussion I had ever witnessed. His hands became invisible for four or five minutes.

Then it happened. A little boy, who looked to be about two or three, got up from his seat on the second row and walked over to the stage. He stared up at the drummer with open-mouthed amazement, his Irish-red hair touching the back of a kelly green T-shirt. As the music ascended, his little body could no longer hold it inside and began to percolate with excitement and then erupted in a highly original dance. His style compensated for his lack of rhythm.

The little boy was oblivious to the crowd. He threw his head even further back and began to twirl in circles. He clapped his hands, stamped his feet, and became a scarecrow in the funnel of a tornado.

The drummer noticed the dancing boy and locked his eyes on him. The boy noticed being noticed, and an instant bond formed. It was as if the two were the only ones present.

The drummer began to play even faster—just for the boy. And the boy danced faster—just for the joy. In one spontaneous moment, a thousand years of cultural history that previously lay dormant in a three-foot-tall body suddenly awakened and rushed out.

In that same moment, I realized what Jesus must have meant when he said all who truly discover the kingdom must do so as a small child. Yes, exactly as this dancing boy. To enter the kingdom is to recognize the cadence of our true culture and step away from where we have been seated. With the glorious freedom of a child, we abandon ourselves to its rhythms and become free from the opinions of others. To enter the kingdom is to become lost in the gaze of the One who is making the music, knowing that it is being played just for you.

Life back inside God's kingdom is so available a child can lead us. We delight in the joy of our true culture. And in the dancing swirl of a few moments of life in the kingdom, letting go replaces grasping, and intimacy trumps isolation.

Becoming lost in God's kingdom brings the freedom of simplicity.

■ Corresponding Freedom

The practice of simplicity brings authenticity and deeper experience of life in the kingdom.

■ Homework Check-Up

If your group has decided to read the corresponding chapters of *Celebration of Discipline* and participate in the daily Scripture readings or transforming exercises as outside-of-class activities, this is the time to do an accountability check and ask for comments concerning the experiences of any participants who would like to share.

D V D

■ Video

In the first segment of this video presentation, Richard Foster provides an introduction to the Discipline of simplicity. He is assisted through a discussion with Glandion Carney and Margaret Campbell.

If your group desires, you can let the DVD continue through a second segment called "Soul Talk" and listen in on a conversation between Richard and Dallas Willard.

■ Central Truths (pp. 50, 51 in Participant's Guide)

You are provided with a few summary points for the teaching section of each video vignette. Here are the Central Truths for the video session about simplicity.

- ■ Simplicity is an inward reality that results from a focus on the kingdom of God.

- ■ Within all of us there is a whole conglomerate of selves vying for attention and dominance. As a result, we often feel distracted, torn, and overcommitted.

- ■ Only when we experience life at the center—where our many selves come under control of the divine arbitrator—do we enter into balance and equilibrium in life.

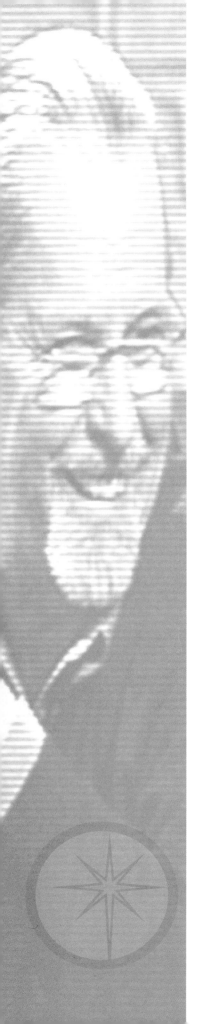

■ Trust that God desires our best interests is at the heart of the inward reality of simplicity.

■ Simplicity is an inward reality that results in an outward lifestyle.

■ Freedom from anxiety is characterized by three inner attitudes:
- If what I have I receive as a gift from God, and
- If what I have is to be cared for by God, and
- If what I have is available to others, then I possess the inward reality of simplicity.

■ Because trust is at the center of a life of simplicity, a good image for the inward reality of simplicity is that of falling back into the arms of Jesus—like a person falling backwards into a swimming pool ("taking the Nestea plunge").

■ Three controlling principles for the outward reality of simplicity are these:
- Buy things for their usefulness rather than their status.
- Reject anything that is producing an addiction in you.
- Develop a habit of giving things away.

(See *Celebration of Discipline*, pp. 90-95, for an expanded listing.)

■ Søren Kierkegaard reminds us that the only reliable path to simplicity is to seek first the kingdom of God.

■ Class Response

Do you have any questions or observations about the video vignettes before we look at the Reflection Questions together?

■ Reflection Questions (p. 51 in Participant's Guide)

Video: Lecture

1 How would seeking the kingdom of God above all else produce the inward reality of simplicity?

2 What are some barriers to seeking the kingdom above all else?

3 Name some of your "many selves" that clamor for attention and make life more complicated. What ways have you explored for attempting to put them under the control of the divine arbitrator?

Book (See *Study Guide for Celebration of Discipline*, p. 41.)

1 What are the three inward attitudes of simplicity? Of the three, which do you find the most difficult for you personally?

2 What is the greatest danger in setting forth an outward expression of Christian simplicity? Why *must* we take the risk?

3 What is producing an addiction in you?

BIBLE STUDY

If time permits, form small groups and allow the participants to complete the Bible study exercise in class.

■ Group Exercise

We will now turn our attention to the Bible for a frame of reference. A brief Bible study can be found on pages 52, 53 in the Participant's Guide and may be used in class or as a homework assignment.

■ Leader's Insight

You may find it helpful to read the entire chapter of Matthew 6—better yet, to read the whole sermon (Matthew 5 through 7)—to provide context for the Bible study in this lesson.

Not only is the "kingdom of God" the primary subject of the Sermon on the Mount; Dallas Willard goes so far as to say, "The gospel is the good news of the presence and availability of life in the kingdom, now and forever, through reliance on Jesus the Anointed" (*The Divine Conspiracy*, p. 49). To better understand this passage (Matthew 6:25-34), it will be helpful to bring three concepts into clearer focus: *duplicity, kingdom of God,* and *righteousness.*

Participant's Guide p. 52

Just before our selected verses, we have the statement from Jesus, "Ye cannot serve God and mammon" (KJV). Although money or wealth is often offered as the meaning of mammon, it is probably more accurate to admit that the precise derivation cannot be determined with complete certainty. It may be more accurate to interpret mammon as anything other than God in which we place our trust (see http://bible.crosswalk.com/Commentaries/JamiesonFaussetBrown/jfb.cgi).

Therefore, immediately prior to Jesus' famous words on freedom from worry and the primary importance of seeking first God's kingdom, he provides an emphatic statement on duplicity. It is impossible to serve both God and substitutes for God.

From this context it may seem that Jesus is simply saying in Matthew 6:25-32, "Don't worry; be happy." But that would be impossible to accomplish even with white-knuckled determination and a case of Xanax. Instead, Jesus is making a case for no duplicity—for simplicity instead.

When it comes to escape from worry, there are three paths, but only one will get us there. Trust can be placed in *mammon*, in substitutes for God. But there is no freedom from anxiety on that road. A person can try to take two paths at the same time, attempting to trust God while holding on to false securities. No good—and very painful. Jesus says that the only path to worry-free living is the simple way of orienting one's entire life around seeking his heavenly kingdom.

But what is the *kingdom of God*?

The kingdom is the range of God's effective will. "Our 'kingdom' is simply *the range of our effective will*. Whatever we genuinely have the say over is in our kingdom" (*The Divine Conspiracy*, p. 21). When Jesus implores his audience to "seek first the kingdom of God," he is, in essence, saying, "Strive to align your will with the will of your Father, and place all your trust in him—instead of in more concrete and temporary God-substitutes."

Concerning the second part of Jesus' challenge—to seek both the kingdom and his (God's) righteousness—it is interesting to observe the following: *Righteousness* connotes a relationship characterized by mutual delight in each other and by loyalty, esteem, and lasting commitment. In a righteous relationship, love defines right behavior toward the other. Righteousness is about joyful surrender of one's will to the will of another—in a mature and loving relationship (see "Righteousness in the Old Testament," *The Interpreter's Dictionary of the Bible*, and *The Molten Soul: Dangers and Opportunities in Religious Conversion*, p. 31).

To seek first God's kingdom and his righteousness is to desire a radical alignment of our will with his—they become one—and a deep, loving, mature, and joyful relationship with him. This is simplicity. This is joy and freedom in Christ.

■ Scripture Meditation

Please note that the Bible Study also includes suggestions for daily Scripture readings (p. 53 in Participant's Guide). Encourage the group participants to spend five to ten minutes with these passages of Scripture each day. As you progress through these sessions, the participants may want to expand this time frame and use these daily passages as part of *lectio divina*.

TRANSFORMING EXERCISES

Please see pages 54, 55 in the Participant's Guide to observe the suggested *Small Group Exercise* and *Individual Exercises*. The *Small Group Exercise* is typically designed for use during your session together. The *Individual Exercises* are based on Dallas Willard's five components of the person and are constructed for the participants to use as homework activities.

SUMMARY

■ Review

Trust that God has our best interests at heart is the key that unlocks the door to simplicity. As we learn to trust God deeply and wholeheartedly, we find it progressively easier to pass through the entry way and step into his kingdom, the realm where the human will becomes one with his will.

■ Richard's Recommendations

Something old: *The Journal and Major Essays of John Woolman*, 1720-1772. (Richmond, IN: Friends United Press, 1989)

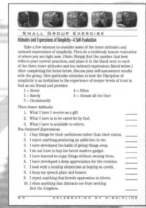

SMALL GROUP

Participant's Guide p. 54

INDIVIDUAL

Participant's Guide p. 55

Something new: *Freedom of Simplicity* by Richard J. Foster.
(San Francisco: HarperSanFrancisco, 1981)

■ Other RENOVARÉ Resources

"Simple Gifts" in *Songs for Renewal* by Janet Lindeblad Janzen
with Richard J. Foster. (San Francisco: HarperSanFrancisco,
1995, p. 94)

A P P E N D I X

Use the appendix that follows to facilitate class exercises and
homework. The *Bible Study, Small Group Exercise*, and *Individual
Exercises* can be found in the Participant's Guide.

Bible Study and Daily Bible Readings
Transforming Exercises (Group and Individual)
Teaching Outline

BIBLE STUDY

Read Matthew 6:25-34.

1 In the verse that immediately precedes our study passage, Jesus says, "You cannot serve God and wealth" ("mammon" in KJV). How would the attempt to trust both God and wealth produce duplicity? What impact would this have on the pursuit of simplicity?

2 In his video presentation, Richard Foster discusses the three inner attitudes of simplicity. What are these attitudes, and what impact would each have on personal anxiety?

3 What does it mean to "seek first the kingdom of God"? How do you orient your life around this teaching of Jesus?

4 What do you think it means to seek God's righteousness?

Daily Scripture Readings

(from *Study Guide for Celebration of Discipline*, pp. 40, 41)

Day	Theme	Passage
Sunday	Simplicity as singleness of heart	Matthew 6:19-24
Monday	Simplicity as trust	Matthew 6:25-34
Tuesday	Simplicity as obedience	Genesis 15
Wednesday	The generosity of simplicity	Leviticus 25:8-12
Thursday	Simplicity in speech	Matthew 5:33-37, James 5:12
Friday	Simplicity and justice	Amos 5:11-15, 24 Luke 4:16-21
Saturday	The freedom from covetousness	Luke 12:13-34

SMALL GROUP EXERCISE

Attitudes and Expressions of Simplicity—A Self-Evaluation

Take a few minutes to consider some of the inner attitudes and outward expressions of simplicity. Then do a ruthlessly honest evaluation of where you are right now. (Note: Simply find the number that best reflects your current practices, and place it in the blank next to each of the three inner attitudes and ten outward expressions listed below.) After completing the items below, discuss your self-assessment results with the group. Give particular attention to how the Discipline of simplicity is an invitation to the experience of deeper levels of trust in God as our friend and provider.

1 = Never   4 = Often
2 = Rarely   5 = Almost all the time
3 = Occasionally

Three Inner Attitudes

1. What I have I receive as a gift.   _____
2. What I have is to be cared for by God.   _____
3. What I have is available to others.   _____

Ten Outward Expressions

1. I buy things for their usefulness rather than their status.   _____
2. I reject anything producing an addiction in me.   _____
3. I have developed the habit of giving things away.   _____
4. I do not have to buy the latest modern gadget.   _____
5. I have learned to enjoy things without owning them.   _____
6. I have developed a deep appreciation for the creation.   _____
7. I look with a healthy skepticism at buying on credit.   _____
8. I keep my speech plain and honest.   _____
9. I reject anything that breeds oppression in others.   _____
10. I shun anything that distracts me from seeking
    first the kingdom.   _____

I N D I V I D U A L   E X E R C I S E

(See *Celebrating the Disciplines: A Journal Workbook to Accompany Celebration of Discipline*, pp. 27-30.)

Thoughts

Commit the Scripture passage, Matthew 6:25-34, to memory this week. Meditate on it, pray over it, and write down any resulting thoughts, insights, or questions in your journal for reflections.

Emotions

Clean out your clothes closet and give away everything you have not worn in a year (with the possible exceptions of a wedding dress or letterman's jacket). Learn from your emotions as you go through the sorting process. What do your feelings teach you? Monitor your emotions again after you give away your extra possessions.

Will

Monitor your attitudes and behavior regarding material possessions as you encounter them in your daily activities this week. Write down your observations.

Behavior

What is something you can do to simplify your life? Tell a friend, and then do it.

Social Interactions

Simply your speech. When you are talking with others, make every attempt to avoid words used either to draw attention to your accomplishments or to flatter the other person.

Teaching Outline

BEFORE YOU LEAD: (TIPS FOR FACILITATOR)

I. INTRODUCTION (WELCOME/PRAYER)

II. WARM-UP (OVERVIEW/FREEDOM/DISCUSSION)

III. DVD (VIDEO/TRUTHS/RESPONSE/REFLECTION)

IV. BIBLE STUDY (INSIGHT/EXERCISE/MEDITATION)

V. EXERCISES (GROUP AND INDIVIDUAL)

VI. SUMMARY (RECOMMENDATIONS/RESOURCES)

Solitude

BEFORE YOU LEAD

Quotes and Quips

Settle yourself in solitude and you will come upon Him in yourself.

Teresa of Avila

God takes this "useless" Discipline, this "wasted time," to make us his friend.

Richard J. Foster

In stillness our false, busy selves are unmasked and seen for the imposters they truly are.

Richard J. Foster

Loneliness is inner emptiness. Solitude is inner fulfillment.

Richard J. Foster

Key Scripture

Thus said the Lord GOD, the Holy One of Israel: In returning and rest you shall be saved; in quietness and in trust shall be your strength...

Isaiah 30:15

■ Note to Leader

If you are using the one-page lesson outlines, you will want to locate that page in the appendix to this lesson or on the CD-ROM now. Please continue to select from the menu of options provided in constructing a lesson tailored to the needs of your group.

■ Materials

For this session *the leader* will need:

- Leader's Guide
- Bible
- DVD Player, Monitor, Stand, Extension Cord, etc.
- *Celebration of Discipline* DVD
- *Celebration of Discipline* (Chapter 7)

For this session *the participant* will need:

- Bible
- Participant's Guide
- Pen or Pencil

SESSION OUTLINE

I. INTRODUCTION
- Welcome
- Prayer

II. WARM-UP
- Overview/Illustration
- Corresponding Freedom
- Discussion of Homework

III. DVD
- Video Vignette
- Central Truths
- Class Response
- Reflection Questions

IV. BIBLE STUDY
- Leader's Insight
- Group Exercise
- Scripture Meditation

V. EXERCISES FOR...
- Small Group Exercise
- Individual Exercises:
  - Thoughts • Emotions • Will
  - Behavior • Social Interactions

VI. SUMMARY
- Richard's Recommendations
- Other RENOVARÉ Resources

INTRODUCTION

■ Welcome

Call the group together and welcome the participants to session seven of *Celebration of Discipline*. Our Discipline for this time together is solitude.

■ Prayer (See *Prayers From the Heart*, p. 36.)

A PRAYER FOR TRANSFORMATION

I PURSUE YOU, JESUS, so that I may be caught by you.
I press in so that I may know your heart.
I stay close so that I may be like you.
Loving Lord, grant me:
    purity of heart,
        humility of soul,
            integrity of life,
                charity for all.

Amen.

WARM-UP

■ Overview and Illustration

I participated in a spiritual retreat several years ago and had a memorable experience with solitude. I went to my first session with the director as an eager pupil. In my briefcase were a Bible and a small library of spiritual classics. After being invited to sit down, I pulled a legal pad from the case and a pen from my pocket and settled into a posture that communicated, *I'm ready for the instructions; just tell me what to do and which of these books to read first.*

To my surprise, the director didn't give me any direction other than, "Go and spend the day alone with God. Enjoy the time with him in silence. We'll talk again tomorrow."

I sat frozen in my chair. My eyes must have been flashing bewilderment as I formed the words, "What? Aren't you going to tell me a bunch of stuff to do? I mean, what's the plan for receiving spiritual nourishment here?"

The director had mercy. "When you were a child, did you ever play by yourself in the back yard?"

"Yes, of course."

"Were you concerned that your parents might forget where you were, or forget to provide a meal for you?"

"Oh, no! I just played."

"Well, that's the way retreats work too. You just go and play with confidence that God is thinking about you and will call to you when it's time to eat."

As a recovering type-A workaholic, I did not make an easy adjustment to the abandonment the director was suggesting. In fact, I cut my time at the monastery short, and it took several more visits before I was able to settle into the play of trust, silence, and solitude. But it was a memorable beginning to a journey that led me to a much deeper appreciation of the fruit found through this Discipline. I'll list my most important discoveries below.

Solitude and Silence

The director told me, in essence, to begin by putting away any agenda of planned activity and control. The goal was simple: be alone with God in silence.

Solitude, I have discovered, requires silence and time alone, but it goes beyond both. Silence and withdrawal from others are the foundation for solitude, but not the edifice itself. As Richard Foster states, we enter solitude "not in order to be away from people, but in order to hear the divine Whisper better" (*Celebration of Discipline*, p. 97).

Dallas Willard provides the following echo: "In solitude we purposefully abstain from interaction with other human beings, denying ourselves companionship and all that comes from our conscious interaction with others. ...Of all the disciplines of abstinence, solitude is generally the most fundamental in the beginning of the spiritual life" (see *The Spirit of the Disciplines: Understanding How God Changes Lives*, pp. 160-163).

Why so? Because when we are quiet enough to hear God's affirming voice, it becomes much easier *not* to fall under the spell of the opinions of others. The primary purpose of solitude is simply to be more present to God.

Trust and Friendship

Although I entered my first retreat experiences with some appreciation for being alone to rest and recharge my batteries, it took me a while to appreciate Richard Foster's keen insight. "In solitude we die to ourselves; we are not trying through solitude to recharge our batteries so we can win the rat race; we are trying to learn to ignore the race altogether" (*Celebration of Discipline Video Series*, Victory Films).

But how can solitude help us ignore all the racing rats and the prize of finishing first? Because in solitude we discover that we are never truly alone. In solitude we discover that the one who made us and loves us most wants to be our friend. He is the prize. Solitude begins with a deep trust that Jesus is present, and it crescendos to a deeper trust that he is a friend who has our best interests at heart.

Furnace of Transformation

But as I have discovered, all is not sweetness and light on the path of solitude. When solitude is most beneficial, it helps to produce the friction of transformation. As Henri Nouwen states, "Solitude is the furnace of transformation…the place of the great struggle and the great encounter—the struggle against the compulsions of the false self [the old man, the Adamic nature], and the encounter with the loving God who offers himself as the substance of the new self [the new man]" (quoted in *Celebrating the Disciplines: A Journal Workbook to Accompany Celebration of Discipline*, p. 34.)

Solitude is a primary Discipline that uses silence and withdrawal as a springboard into both a deepening relationship with God and the furnace of transformation.

■ Corresponding Freedoms

Solitude encourages serenity, increased love of God and others, and unmasking of the false self.

■ Homework Check-Up

If your group has decided to read the corresponding chapters of *Celebration of Discipline* and participate in the daily Scripture readings or transforming exercises as outside-of-class activities, this is the time to do an accountability check and ask for comments concerning the experiences of any participants who would like to share.

DVD

■ Video

In the first segment of this video presentation, Richard Foster provides an introduction to the Discipline of solitude. He is assisted through a discussion with Glandion Carney and Margaret Campbell.

If your group desires, you can let the DVD continue through a second segment called "Soul Talk" and listen in on a conversation between Richard and Dallas Willard.

■ Central Truths (pp. 56, 57 in Participant's Guide)

You are provided with a few summary points for the teaching section of each video vignette. Here are the Central Truths for the video session about solitude.

- Whereas prayer is the most central of the Disciplines of engagement, the *via positiva*, solitude is the most central of the Disciplines of abstinence, the *via negativa*.

- Solitude creates an open, empty space where we can be found by God and let go of all competing loyalties.

- Thomas Merton says, "It is in deep solitude that I can find the gentleness with which to love others."

- Solitude and silence teach me to love others for who they are, not what they say.

- We need the balance of both solitude and community.

- In solitude we are not attempting to recharge our batteries so we can win the rat race; in solitude we learn to ignore the rat race altogether.

- Solitude can help us learn to be present where we are.

- As we learn to die to ourselves, we can come alive in God.

■ Class Response

Do you have any questions or observations about the video vignettes before we look at the Reflection Questions together?

■ Reflection Questions (p. 57 in Participant's Guide)

Video: Lecture

1 Are you aware of any barriers to your experience of solitude? Which of these (either internal or external) can you overcome?

2 What do you make of Thomas Merton's statement that in solitude a person can find the gentleness with which to love others?

3 How can solitude help create an open space for God? How does it help you learn to ignore the rat race?

Book (from *Study Guide for Celebration of Discipline*, p. 46)

1 What is the difference between loneliness and solitude? Which do you experience more?

2 Why do you think that solitude and silence are closely connected?

3 What experience in solitude would you like to have two years from now that you do not presently possess?

BIBLE STUDY

If time permits, form small groups and allow the participants to complete the Bible study exercise in class.

■ Group Exercise

We will now turn our attention to the Bible for a frame of reference. A brief Bible study can be found on pages 58, 59 in the Participant's Guide and may be used in class or as a homework assignment.

BIBLE STUDY

Participant's Guide p. 58

■ Leader's Insight

Ephesians is different from many other letters from Paul in that it is not focused on a particular problem in the church. Instead, Paul wrote to provide a better understanding of God's higher goals and purpose—to bring praise and glory to God through demonstrating reconciliation and unity with others.

In the passage we are examining in the Bible study (Ephesians 3:14-21), Paul is offering a prayer that the Christians of Ephesus will have a deeper experience of God's fullness. And how does a person become "filled with all the fullness of God"? Paul's suggestions are very straightforward. We become full of God as we are strengthened in our inner being with power through (Christ's) Spirit and allow Christ to dwell in our hearts through faith, thereby becoming rooted and grounded in love.

The present passage is a prayer for Christian formation. Christians become full of God as we yield our insides to the transforming presence of Christ. In solitude it becomes easier to hear God's whisper about his highest purpose for our lives—to be overflowing with the loving presence of Christ.

■ Scripture Meditation

Please note that the Bible Study also includes suggestions for daily Scripture readings (p. 59 in Participant's Guide). Encourage the group participants to spend five to ten minutes with these passages of Scripture each day. As you progress through these sessions, the participants may want to expand this time frame and use these daily passages as part of *lectio divina*.

TRANSFORMING EXERCISES

Please see pages 60-63 in the Participant's Guide to observe the suggested *Small Group Exercise* and *Individual Exercises*. The *Small Group Exercise* is typically designed for use during your session together. The *Individual Exercises* are based on Dallas Willard's five components of the person and are constructed for the participants to use as homework activities.

SMALL GROUP

Participant's Guide p. 60

INDIVIDUAL

Participant's Guide p. 62

SUMMARY

■ Review

Solitude is one of the most foundational of all the Christian Disciplines. In solitude we learn to unplug from the noise and crowds of the world for the purpose of being with God and learning to hear his voice better. In solitude we become free from the compulsion of pleasing others—and our own desires—so that we can better please God. And in this "wasted time" of solitude, God's whispered secret is often heard. He longs to make us his friend.

■ Richard's Recommendations

Something old: *The Sayings of the Desert Fathers*, 4th-6th centuries. (Kalamazoo, MI: Cistercian Publications, 1987)

Something new: *Out of Solitude* by Henri Nouwen. (Notre Dame, IN: Ave Maria, 1974)

■ Other RENOVARÉ Resources

Wilderness Time by Emilie Griffin. (San Francisco: HarperSanFrancisco, 1997)

APPENDIX

Use the appendix that follows to facilitate class exercises and homework. The *Bible Study, Small Group Exercise*, and *Individual Exercises* can be found in the Participant's Guide.

Bible Study and Daily Bible Readings
Transforming Exercises (Group and Individual)
Teaching Outline

BIBLE STUDY

Read Ephesians 3:14-21.

1 Ephesians 3:14-21 is sometimes referred to as Paul's prayer for the Ephesians. Please read these verses through a second time. In just a few words, how would you summarize Paul's desires for the Christians at Ephesus?

2 What does it mean to "be filled with all the fullness of God"? Is this an experience to which you can relate? What has it been like for you?

3 Paul may be indicating that to be filled with God requires becoming "rooted and grounded in love" (see verse 17). What role does the Discipline of solitude play in this process?

4 How can you change the structure of your day to incorporate more practice with silence and solitude for the purpose of being more filled with the fullness of God?

Daily Scripture Readings

(from *Study Guide for Celebration of Discipline*, pp. 45, 46)

Day	*Theme*	*Passage*
Sunday	The freedom to control the tongue	James 3:1-12; Luke 23:6-9
Monday	Prayer and solitude	Matthew 6:5-6; Luke 5:16
Tuesday	The insights of solitude	Psalm 8
Wednesday	"The dark night of the soul"	Jeremiah 20:7-18
Thursday	The solitude of the garden	Matthew 26:36-46
Friday	The solitude of the cross	Matthew 27:32-50
Saturday	The compassion that comes from solitude	Matthew 9:35-38, 23:37

SMALL GROUP EXERCISE

Steps Into Solitude

In *Celebration of Discipline* Richard Foster describes seven practical steps for beginning the Discipline of solitude. These steps are summarized below. Please enjoy ten minutes of silence for reflecting on each of these practical suggestions. For each step, please write down some ideas for ways to incorporate the activity into the routine of your life.

SEVEN STEPS INTO SOLITUDE

1. *I can learn to take advantage of the "little solitudes" that fill my day (e.g., early morning moments in bed, a morning cup of coffee).* List other "little solitudes" available to you each day.

   _____

   _____

   _____

2. *I can develop a "quiet place" designed for silence and solitude.* Think of the best place inside your home that can be used as a quiet place—and pick the best time of the day for your "mini-retreat."

   _____

   _____

   _____

3. *I can find a place outside the home (e.g., a spot in the park, a church sanctuary that is kept unlocked, even a storage closet somewhere) for solitude.* Describe this place.

   _____

_____

_____

4. *I can experiment with doing deeds without any words of explanation—avoiding the use of words in a frantic attempt to explain or justify my actions.* What are some specific things you can do (in silence) for others this week?

_____

_____

_____

5. *I can maintain plain speech—using words that are few and full.* Resolve to reduce the volume of words used this week.

_____

_____

_____

6. *I can try to live one entire day this week without words.* Decide which day (or part of a day) would work best for you.

_____

_____

_____

7. *I can withdraw for three or four hours for the purpose of reorienting my life goals.* Pick a time period (one morning, afternoon, or evening) for reevaluating your goals and objectives in life. Give yourself bonus points if you can do so during the next week.

_____

_____

_____

INDIVIDUAL EXERCISES

(See *Celebrating the Disciplines: A Journal Workbook to Accompany Celebration of Discipline*, pp. 34.)

Thoughts

Take five minutes each day this week for a time of silent reflection on one of the following verses (selected from the Spiritual Index of *The RENOVARÉ Study Bible*.)

Numbers 23:9 From the top of the crags I see him, from the hills I behold him; Here is a people living alone, and not reckoning itself among the nations!

Psalms 62:5 For God alone my soul waits in silence, for my hope is from him.

Matthew 14:23 After he had dismissed the crowds, he went up the mountain by himself to pray. When evening came, he was there alone.

Mark 1:35 In the morning, while it was still very dark, he got up and went out to a deserted place, and there he prayed.

Mark 6:31 Come away to a deserted place all by yourselves and rest a while.

John 16:32 The hour is coming, indeed it has come, when…you will leave me alone. Yet I am not alone because the Father is with me.

Galatians 1:17-22 …I went away at once into Arabia….

62   CELEBRATION OF DISCIPLINE

Emotions

Be alert to any longings for solitude that you experience this week. Write down the circumstances surrounding those longings, and consider what prompted them. What do they indicate about your need to practice the Discipline of solitude?

Will

Take a day for enjoying each of the "little solitudes" you have identified. Write down in journal entries when and where you found opportunities, how you spent them, and what differences they made in your day or week.

Behavior

Spend a session in the "quiet place" you have identified. Focus on the fruitfulness of silence.

Social Interactions

Spend a day or part of a day without words.

Teaching Outline

BEFORE YOU LEAD: (TIPS FOR FACILITATOR)

I. INTRODUCTION (WELCOME/PRAYER)

II. WARM-UP (OVERVIEW/FREEDOM/DISCUSSION)

III. DVD (VIDEO/TRUTHS/RESPONSE/REFLECTION)

IV. BIBLE STUDY (INSIGHT/EXERCISE/MEDITATION)

V. EXERCISES (GROUP AND INDIVIDUAL)

VI. SUMMARY (RECOMMENDATIONS/RESOURCES)

SESSION EIGHT:
Submission

BEFORE YOU LEAD

◼ Quotes and Quips

A Christian is a perfectly free lord of all, subject to none. A Christian is a perfectly dutiful servant of all, subject to all.

Martin Luther

The most radical social teaching of Jesus was his total reversal of the contemporary notion of greatness. Leadership is found in becoming a servant of all. Power is discovered in submission. The foremost symbol of this radical servanthood is the cross.

Richard J. Foster

In reality, Jesus' teaching on self-denial is the only thing that will bring genuine self-fulfillment and self-actualization.

Richard J. Foster

◼ Key Scriptures

He called the crowd with his disciples, and said to them, "If any want to become my followers, let them deny themselves and take up their cross and follow me."

Mark 8:34

Be subject to one another out of reverence for Christ.

Ephesians 5:21

■ Note to Leader

If you are using the one-page lesson outlines, you will want to locate that page in the appendix to this lesson or on the CD-ROM now. Please continue to select from the menu of options provided in constructing a lesson tailored to the needs of your group.

■ Materials

For this session *the leader* will need:

- Leader's Guide
- Bible
- DVD Player, Monitor, Stand, Extension Cord, etc.
- *Celebration of Discipline* DVD
- *Celebration of Discipline* (Chapter 8)

For this session *the participant* will need:

- Bible
- Participant's Guide
- Pen or Pencil

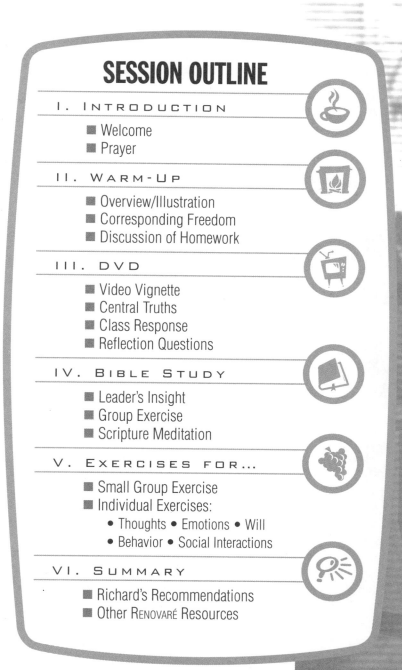

SESSION OUTLINE

I. INTRODUCTION
- Welcome
- Prayer

II. WARM-UP
- Overview/Illustration
- Corresponding Freedom
- Discussion of Homework

III. DVD
- Video Vignette
- Central Truths
- Class Response
- Reflection Questions

IV. BIBLE STUDY
- Leader's Insight
- Group Exercise
- Scripture Meditation

V. EXERCISES FOR...
- Small Group Exercise
- Individual Exercises:
  - Thoughts • Emotions • Will
  - Behavior • Social Interactions

VI. SUMMARY
- Richard's Recommendations
- Other RENOVARÉ Resources

INTRODUCTION

■ Welcome

Call the group together and welcome the participants to session eight of *Celebration of Discipline*. Our Discipline for this time together is submission.

■ Prayer (See *Prayers From the Heart*, p. 26.)

A PRAYER OF SELF-EMPTYING

Loving God, I choose this day to be a servant. I yield my right to command and demand. I give up my need to manage and control. I relinquish all schemes of manipulation and exploitation.
For Jesus' sake,
Amen.

WARM-UP

■ Overview and Illustration (from *Falling for God*, pp. 95, 96)

Our family has watched the movie *The Princess Bride* so many times we've accidentally memorized most of the dialogue. As the story begins, we see the heroine going about chores on a farm. Her name is Buttercup (I know, but I still like the movie). Soon we meet a young man who works on the farm and answers to the name Farm Boy.

Whenever Buttercup asks Farm Boy to do something for her, he always replies, "As you wish." And that's all he ever says to her.

As they grow into their hormones, Buttercup seems to be developing a crush on Farm Boy. One day as he is about to leave the room, she asks him to fetch a pitcher that is within easy reach for her. Farm Boy walks over, while staring into her eyes. He lifts the pitcher and says, "As you wish," in a breathy whisper.

And in that moment, returning his gaze, Buttercup realizes that every time he has said, "As you wish," he was really saying, "I love you." The next scene is, of course, a romantic kiss that became the poster shot for the movie.

Submission means saying "As you wish" to God. It is another way of saying "I love you."

From a much less romanticized vantage point, submission is also the Discipline through which we experience Jesus' shocking statement in Mark 8:34: "If any want to become my followers, let them deny themselves and take up their cross and follow me."

Now consider the emotions you experienced while reading the above. If you are like me, you felt drawn toward the story of Farm Boy and Buttercup, inspired by the notion of saying "As you wish" as an act of love. But you may have felt repulsed by the notion of being nailed to your own personal cross. Come on, let's be honest. Who wants radical self-denial when self-fulfillment is in view?

Is it any wonder it is so common to attempt to practice a form of Christianity that is free from personal crosses and the language of self-denial? Is it surprising that the foundational Discipline of submission is so often either ignored or turned inside out—perverted into some form of imposing one's will on a codependent other? (Please read chapter 8 of *Celebration of Discipline* for an excellent treatment of the ways submission is often abused.)

In *Celebration of Discipline,* Richard Foster makes the bold statement, "In reality, Jesus' teaching on self-denial [submission] is the only thing that will bring genuine self-fulfillment and self-actualization" (p. 113). Yes, Jesus knew the great secret to human freedom and joy. We are not instructed to pick up our own personal cross to glorify masochistic suffering or to earn salvation. We embrace self-denial as the Discipline of submission because it is the path to self-fulfillment. Submission means saying "As you wish" to God as an act of supreme love. And with his help, we learn to say "As you wish" to others too.

Corresponding Freedom

Submission gives us (1) the ability to lay down the terrible burden of always needing to get our own way and (2) the freedom to love people unconditionally.

Homework Check-Up

If your group has decided to read the corresponding chapters of *Celebration of Discipline* and participate in the daily Scripture readings or transforming exercises as outside-of-class activities, this is the time to do an accountability check and ask for comments

concerning the experiences of any participants who would like to share.

DVD

■ Video

In the first segment of this video presentation, Richard Foster provides an introduction to the Discipline of submission. He is assisted through a discussion with Glandion Carney, Margaret Campbell, and Jeff and DeAnne Terrell.

If your group desires, you can let the DVD continue through a second segment called "Soul Talk" and listen in on a conversation between Richard and Dallas Willard.

■ Central Truths (pp. 64, 65 in Participant's Guide)

You are provided with a few summary points for the teaching section of each video vignette. Here are the Central Truths for the video session about submission.

■ "We have seen and known some people who seem to have found this deep Center of living, where the fretful calls of life are integrated, where no as well as yes can be said with confidence." (Thomas Kelly, *Testament of Devotion*, p. viii)

■ Richard's encounter with Thomas Kelly's words led to a covenant commitment with God to live out of a Divine center, submitting to the will of God, the needs of his family, and his own human limitations.

■ Submission is learning to say yes and no with confidence.

■ Submission is the most abused of all the Spiritual Disciplines.

■ Submission is not putting another under our authority. Submission is laying down the terrible burden of always needing to get our own way.

■ Paul crystallized the notion of submission in Ephesians 5:21, where he wrote, "Be subject to one another out of reverence for Christ."

■ Submission is not a natural process, but a supernatural process.

■ True submission is not in the details of who gets his or her way, but in an attitude toward the beloved.

■ There are seven acts of submission (see *Celebration of Discipline*, pp. 122, 123):

1. ...to the Triune God
2. ...to the Scripture
3. ...to our family
4. ...to our neighbors
5. ...to the believing community
6. ...to the broken and despised
7. ...to the world

■ Class Response

Do you have any questions or observations about the video vignettes before we look at the Reflection Questions together?

■ Reflection Questions (p. 65 in Participant's Guide)

Video: Lecture

1 What does the Discipline of submission have to do with finding what Thomas Kelly calls "this deep Center of living"?

2 Why do you believe submission is the most abused of all the Christian Disciplines?

3 If Ephesians 5:21 ("Be subject to one another out of reverence for Christ") is taken seriously, how will it change the way you live your life?

Book (See *Study Guide for Celebration of Discipline*, pp. 50, 51.)

1 How have you seen the Discipline of submission abused?

2 What images come to your mind when you think of the word *self-denial*?

3 What are the limits of submission, and why are they important? (Hint: see *Celebration of Discipline*, pp. 120, 121.)

BIBLE STUDY

If time permits, form small groups and allow the participants to complete the Bible study exercise in class.

■ Group Exercise

We will now turn our attention to the Bible as a frame of reference. A brief Bible study can be found on pages 66, 67 in the Participant's Guide and may be used in class or as a homework assignment.

■ Leader's Insight

In Lewis Smedes' book *Union With Christ*, he observes that the apostle Paul uses the phrase "in Christ" 164 times. Arguably, it is the number one theme in Paul's writing. In his teaching, "united in Christ" refers to the personal union of the believer with Jesus and is the essential reality of salvation. To be in Christ is to be saved (see commentary on Philippians 2:1 of the *NIV Study Bible*). It is from this intimate and personal relationship with Jesus—being organically connected to him—that the benefits of salvation flow from the life of the believer.

Only by yielding to the indwelling presence of Christ can the believer become like-minded with him and live in harmony with other believers. It is not a matter of trying to figure out what Jesus

Participant's Guide p. 66

would be thinking and then, with white-knuckled determination, to begin placing those thoughts in our minds. No, we take on the mind of Christ by opening the deepest recesses of our being to his living presence. We don't will ourselves to think Christ's thoughts; we will ourselves to allow Jesus to live his life through us.

As we yield to union with Christ, his attitude—the self-sacrificing humility of a servant—becomes our attitude. And this process of continually yielding to Christ is the personal cross that Jesus instructs us to embrace. Denial of self-rule and submitting to the rule of the indwelling Christ is the great secret of self-fulfillment and the Discipline of submission.

■ Scripture Meditation

Please note that the Bible Study also includes suggestions for daily Scripture readings (p. 67 in Participant's Guide). Encourage the group participants to spend five to ten minutes with these passages of Scripture each day. As you progress through these sessions, the participants may want to expand this time frame and use these daily passages as part of *lectio divina*.

TRANSFORMING EXERCISES

Please see pages 68-71 in the Participant's Guide to observe the suggested *Small Group Exercise* and *Individual Exercises*. The *Small Group Exercise* is typically designed for use during your session together. The *Individual Exercises* are based on Dallas Willard's five components of the person and are constructed for the participants to use as homework activities.

SUMMARY

■ Review

According to Richard Foster, submission is the most abused of all the Christian Disciplines. But it also the path that leads to taking on the mind (thoughts and emotions), behavior, will, and social relations of Christ as we surrender our insides to his transforming presence. In submission we learn that self-denial is the way to self-fulfillment.

SMALL GROUP

Participant's Guide p. 68

INDIVIDUAL

Participant's Guide p. 70

■ Richard's Recommendations

Something old: *The Bondage of the Will* by Martin Luther, 1483-1546. (Nashville, TN: Revell, 1990)

Something new: *The Politics of Jesus* by John Howard Yoder. (Grand Rapids, MI: Eerdmans, 1994)

■ Other Renovaré Resources

Spiritual Classics edited by Emilie Griffin and Richard J. Foster. (San Francisco, Harper San Francisco, 2000, pp. 171-196)

A P P E N D I X

Use the appendix that follows to facilitate class exercises and homework. The *Bible Study, Small Group Exercise*, and *Individual Exercises* can be found in the Participant's Guide.

> *Bible Study and Daily Bible Readings*
> *Transforming Exercises (Group and Individual)*
> *Teaching Outline*

BIBLE STUDY

Read Philippians 2:1-11.

① What does this passage teach you about submission?

② What do you think Paul means when he says, "Let the same mind be in you that was in Christ Jesus" (Philippians 2:5)?

③ How would you advise someone who wanted to have the mind of Christ? What works in your own life?

④ Paul states that Jesus, our example of humility and submission, "became obedient to the point of death—even death on a cross" (see Philippians 2:8). How does this relate to Jesus' injunction in Mark 8:34 ("If any want to become my followers, let them deny themselves and take up their cross and follow me")?

⑤ How would you explain the difference between self-denial and self-rejection?

Daily Scripture Readings

(from *Study Guide for Celebration of Discipline*, p. 50)

Day	Theme	Passage
Sunday	The call to submission	Mark 8:34, John 12:24-26
Monday	The example of Christ	Philippians 2:1-11
Tuesday	The example of Abraham	Genesis 22:1-19
Wednesday	The example of Paul	Galatians 2:19-21
Thursday	Submission in the marketplace	Matthew 5:38-48
Friday	Submission in the family	Ephesians 5:21-6:9, 1 Peter 3:1-9
Saturday	Submission with reference to the state	Romans 13:1-10, Acts 4:13-20, 5:27-29, 16:35-39

SMALL GROUP EXERCISE

Seven Areas of Submission

(See *Celebrating the Disciplines: A Journal Workbook to Accompany Celebration of Discipline*, p. 144.)

Review the seven areas in which Richard Foster suggests we are to practice submission: to the Triune God, to the Scripture, to our family, to our neighbors and acquaintances, to the believing community, to the helpless and outcast of our society, and to the world as international community. Choose one of these areas in which to focus your practice of submission. Other Disciplines can be helpful here. For example:

- Spend ten to fifteen minutes each morning in listening prayer as you submit the coming day to God's purposes.

- Submit yourself to the Scripture by hearing it preached in worship. Then reflect on the same text in your own sessions of meditative reading and study. Make it your goal to hear, receive, and obey the Word.

- Submit to the interests of others in your family community by taking time to listen carefully to family members.

- Look for small, hidden acts of service you can perform for neighbors and acquaintances.

- Volunteer for a task in your community of faith. Submit to the needs of the group without looking for recognition or position.

- Submit to the needs of the abandoned and helpless persons in society. Whether in intercession or direct service, look for ways to sacrifice your own interests in identification with them.

■ Choose a way to participate responsibly in meeting global needs. Seek God's leading for how you should practice submission as a member of the world community.

After taking some time to settle on a particular area and method (you may choose to modify one of the above suggestions), please share with the group how you plan to make the Discipline of submission more real in your life during the coming week.

I N D I V I D U A L   E X E R C I S E S

(See *Celebrating the Disciplines: A Journal Workbook to Accompany Celebration of Discipline*, p. 39.)

Thoughts

Clarify your points of agreement or disagreement with the material presented in this session.

Emotions

Spend a few moments listening to your emotions as you reflect on the notion of submission in your own life. Take some notes on what your emotions have to teach you. Do they seem to be signals that remind you of abuses of submission that you have either observed or experienced? Do they signal a deep longing for union with Christ? Is there something else they signal as you think about the Discipline of submission? Ask God to show you what to do with the information your emotions provide.

Will

Take a few minutes each day this week to slowly breathe the following prayer by Ignatius of Loyola (see *Prayers From the Heart*, p. 27).

I SURRENDER ALL TO YOUR DIVINE WILL

TAKE, LORD, all my liberty,
my memory, my understanding
and my whole will.
You have given me all that I have,
all that I am,
and I surrender all to Your Divine will.

You have given me all that I have,
all that I am,
and I surrender all to Your Divine will.
Give me only Your love and Your grace.
With this I am rich enough,
and I have no more to ask.
Amen.

Behavior

Make a list of opportunities you have daily to give up your own rights for the good of others, and choose one opportunity on which to act this week.

Social Interactions

Take questions and concerns about submission or self-denial to one or more people you respect and trust. Ask them to talk through these issues with you. Take notes if it is comfortable to do so, and afterward write down a summary of reflections.

Teaching Outline

BEFORE YOU LEAD: (TIPS FOR FACILITATOR)

I. INTRODUCTION (WELCOME/PRAYER)

II. WARM-UP (OVERVIEW/FREEDOM/DISCUSSION)

III. DVD (VIDEO/TRUTHS/RESPONSE/REFLECTION)

IV. BIBLE STUDY (INSIGHT/EXERCISE/MEDITATION)

V. EXERCISES (GROUP AND INDIVIDUAL)

VI. SUMMARY (RECOMMENDATIONS/RESOURCES)

SESSION NINE:
Service

BEFORE YOU LEAD

■ Quotes and Quips

As the cross is the sign of submission, so the towel is the sign of service.

Richard J. Foster

Learn the lesson that, if you want to do the work of the prophet, what you need is not a scepter but a hoe.

Bernard of Clairvaux

We are called to serve through the many little deaths of going beyond self. And as we live our lives for the good of others, amazingly, we find ourselves....

Richard J. Foster

■ Key Scriptures

...Whoever wishes to be great among you must be your servant.

Matthew 20:26

...I am among you as one who serves.

Luke 22:27

■ Note to Leader

If you are using the one-page lesson outlines, you will want to locate that page in the appendix to this lesson or on the CD-ROM now. Please continue to select from the menu of options provided in constructing a lesson tailored to the needs of your group.

■ Materials

For this session *the leader* will need:

- Leader's Guide
- Bible
- DVD Player, Monitor, Stand, Extension Cord, etc.
- *Celebration of Discipline* DVD
- *Celebration of Discipline* (Chapter 9)

For this session *the participant* will need:

- Bible
- Participant's Guide
- Pen or Pencil

SESSION OUTLINE

I. INTRODUCTION
- Welcome
- Prayer

II. WARM-UP
- Overview/Illustration
- Corresponding Freedom
- Discussion of Homework

III. DVD
- Video Vignette
- Central Truths
- Class Response
- Reflection Questions

IV. BIBLE STUDY
- Leader's Insight
- Group Exercise
- Scripture Meditation

V. EXERCISES FOR...
- Small Group Exercise
- Individual Exercises:
  - Thoughts • Emotions • Will
  - Behavior • Social Interactions

VI. SUMMARY
- Richard's Recommendations
- Other RENOVARÉ Resources

INTRODUCTION

■ Welcome

Call your group together and welcome the participants to session nine of *Celebration of Discipline*. Our Discipline for this time together is service.

■ Prayer (See *Prayers From the Heart*, p. 83.)

MAY I SEE YOU TODAY

Dearest Lord, may I see you today and every day in the person of your sick, and, while nursing them, minister unto you. Though you hide yourself behind the unattractive disguise of the irritable, the exacting, the unreasonable, may I still recognize you, and say: "Jesus, my patient, how sweet it is to serve you."

Mother Teresa of Calcutta

WARM-UP

■ Overview and Illustration

In 1948, Agnes Gonxha Bojaxhiu came across a half-dead woman lying in front of a hospital. Unable to obtain medical treatment for the poor woman, Agnes stayed with her until she died. And from that point on, Ms. Bojaxhiu—now better known as Mother Teresa—dedicated her life to the "call within a call" that God had whispered into her heart two years prior. She became a servant to the poorest of the poor in India, eventually earning a second title, "Saint of the Gutters. "

Mother Teresa's life story became a script that stretches the boundaries of credulity. The quiet, diminutive, and somewhat homely nun was a living icon of service. Amid the stench of leprosy and soiled linen, open sores and hand-closed eyes, Mother Teresa drew the gaze of the world and was showered with scores of awards, including an honorary Ph.D. from Cambridge and the Nobel Peace Prize.

Her approach to ministry inspired over 4,000 women to give

their lives to serving the poor. Her Missionaries of Charity grew at an astonishing rate. Today her order is present in 80 countries, feeding 500,000 families and helping almost 100,000 lepers every year. (Read more about Mother Teresa at http://www.catholic.net/hope_healing/ template_channel.phtml?channel_id=22.)

What is the secret to her ministry? I believe it is as simple as it is moving. In her own oft-quoted words, "I see God in every human being. When I wash the leper's wounds, I feel I am nursing the Lord himself. Is it not a beautiful experience?"

Yes it is, and her approach to service is echoed in the words of Richard Foster. He says in *Celebration of Discipline* (p. 128), "True service comes from a relationship with the divine Other deep inside. We serve out of whispered promptings, divine urgings."

Yes, service requires highly sensitive ears and eyes. True servants of God are able to hear his divine whisper and see, in the eyes of those we serve, the eyes of Jesus. This will take some practice; perhaps I need to begin with family, friends, and colleagues and see where this journey of love will lead.

■ Corresponding Freedom

Service abolishes our need (and desire) for a "pecking order," and, more than any other Discipline, service works the grace of humility into our lives.

■ Homework Check-Up

If your group has decided to read the corresponding chapters of *Celebration of Discipline* and participate in the daily Scripture readings or transforming exercises as outside-of-class activities, this is the time to do an accountability check and ask for comments concerning the experiences of any participants who would like to share.

DVD

■ Video

In the first segment of this video presentation, Richard Foster provides an introduction to the Discipline of service. He is assisted through a discussion with Glandion Carney and Margaret Campbell.

If your group desires, you can let the DVD continue through a second segment called "Soul Talk" and listen in on a conversation between Richard and Dallas Willard.

■ Central Truths (pp. 72, 73 in Participant's Guide)

You are provided with a few summary points for the teaching section of each video vignette. Here are the Central Truths for the video session about service.

■ "Active helpfulness...means, initially, simple assistance in trifling, external matters....One who worries about the loss of time that such petty, outward acts of helpfulness entail is usually taking the importance of his own career too solemnly" (Dietrich Bonhoeffer, *Life Together*, quoted in *Celebration of Discipline*, p. 135).

■ Whereas the cross is the sign of submission, the towel is the sign of service.

■ Jesus helped his disciples resolve the issue of who was the greatest among them by washing their feet, thus reinterpreting the meaning of greatness.

■ Service is the Discipline of the many "little deaths" of going beyond ourselves, and it has to work itself out in practical life.

■ The grace of God empowers us to move beyond ourselves and into service.

■ Differences between self-righteous service and true service:

■ Self-righteous service

1. Comes through human effort.
2. Is impressed with the big deal.
3. Requires external rewards.
4. Is highly concerned about results.
5. Picks and chooses whom to serve.
6. Is affected by moods and whims.
7. Is temporary.
8. Is insensitive and insists on meeting a need.
9. Fractures community.

- True Service
    1. Comes from a relationship with the divine Other deep inside.
    2. Finds it almost impossible to distinguish the small from the large service.
    3. Rests contented in hiddenness.
    4. Is free of the need to calculate results.
    5. Is indiscriminate in its ministry.
    6. Ministers simply and faithfully because there is a need.
    7. Is a lifestyle.
    8. Can withhold the service as freely as perform it.
    9. Builds community.

- To arrive at true service, we must get beyond the feeling that we deserve a reward for our efforts for others.

- A way to become more involved in the Discipline of service would be to pray each day, "Lord, lead me today to somebody whom I can serve."

Class Response

Do you have any questions or observations about the video vignettes before we look at the Reflection Questions together?

Reflection Questions (p. 73 in Participant's Guide)

Video: Lecture

1 Have you ever experienced anything like what Richard described—serving someone while cursing your luck that you were not able to be working on some other project? How did your story end?

2 What do you think about the way Jesus modeled the reinterpretation of what it means to be great? As you attempt to follow Jesus' example of what it means to be great, what obstacles are most difficult for you to overcome?

❸ What seems to be at the heart of the difference between self-righteous service and true service?

Book (See *Study Guide for Celebration of Discipline*, pp. 54, 55.)

❶ If the towel is the sign of service, how can that sign be manifested in twenty-first-century culture?

❷ In *Celebration of Discipline* Richard Foster mentions that service works humility into our lives. What in the world do you think *humility* means? That is, what does humility look like?

❸ Give this prayer a try sometime this month: "Lord Jesus, I would greatly appreciate it if you would bring me someone today whom I can serve." (Question 3 not in Participant's Guide)

BIBLE STUDY

If time permits, form small groups and allow the participants to complete the Bible study exercise in class.

■ Group Exercise

We will now turn our attention to the Bible as a frame of reference. A brief Bible study can be found on pages 74, 75 in the Participant's Guide and may be used in class or as a homework assignment.

■ Leader's Insight

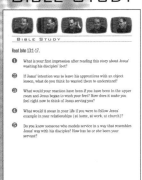

Participant's Guide p. 74

In chapter three we considered Jesus' last night with his disciples (see John 13-17) and prayer as a way of staying connected to God, the way branches stay connected to a vine. Let's return to that amazing night.

How did Jesus begin? By taking off his outer clothing and wrapping a towel around his waist. He began his farewell address by pouring himself out, washing the dirty feet of his disciples. The King of kings knelt to take on the posture of a servant. No, lower than a servant. In that day a servant with any clout would resist such a humiliating chore. Greatness and leadership were forever redefined.

Were his only teaching points humility and service? No, that was just the introduction. Careful reading of the Gospel of John reveals that Jesus' primary emphasis in chapters 13 through 17 was love and unity.

Although the word *love* occurs only 6 times in chapters 1 through 12, Jesus refers to love 31 times during his farewell address (see *NIV Study Bible* commentary on John 13). Thirty-one times Jesus refers to the supreme injunction to love. But even love is not the crescendo point; Jesus' commencement address ends with a prayer for his disciples, and his prayer ends with an appeal to his Father, an appeal that refers to you:

"My prayer is not for them alone. I pray also for those who will believe in me through their message, that all of them may be one, Father, just as you are in me and I am in you. May they also be in us so that the world may believe that you have sent me. I have given them the glory that you gave me, that they may be one as we are one: I in them and you in me...." (John 17:20-23, NIV)

What powerful images: Jesus with a towel, the first communion, vines and branches, the supreme spiritual fruit of love, living in unity with one another and with God.

Service softens the heart, removing the barriers of pride and selfishness so that love can flow in from God and back out to others. Without true service there is no love and no union. The lesson was so important, Jesus stooped low to make sure his disciples would understand his words.

■ Scripture Meditation

Please note that the Bible Study also includes suggestions for daily Scripture readings (p. 75 in Participant's Guide). Encourage the group participants to spend five to ten minutes with these passages of Scripture each day. As you progress through these sessions, the participants may want to expand this time frame and use these daily passages as part of *lectio divina*.

TRANSFORMING EXERCISES

Please see pages 76-79 in the Participant's Guide to observe the suggested *Small Group Exercise* and *Individual Exercises*. The *Small Group Exercise* is typically designed for use during your session together. The *Individual Exercises* are based on Dallas

SMALL GROUP

Participant's Guide p. 76

INDIVIDUAL

Participant's Guide p. 78

Willard's five components of the person and are constructed for the participants to use as homework activities.

SUMMARY

■ Review

Richard Foster provides a concise summary of the Discipline of service when he writes: "True service comes from a relationship with the divine Other deep inside. We serve out of whispered promptings, divine urges. Energy is expended but it is not the frantic energy of the flesh." (*Celebration of Discipline*, p. 128) In true service we both see Jesus in the faces of those we serve and become a conduit for his love.

■ Richard's Recommendations

Something old: *The Rule of St. Benedict: 12 Steps Into Humility*, 6th century. (New York: Vintage, 1998)

Something new: *Servant Leadership* by Robert K. Greenleaf. (Mahwah, NJ: Paulist, 2002)

■ Other RENOVARÉ Resources

Streams of Living Water by Richard J. Foster. (San Francisco: HarperSanFrancisco, 1998, pp. 134-183)

APPENDIX

Use the appendix that follows to facilitate class exercises and homework. The *Bible Study, Small Group Exercise*, and *Individual Exercises* can be found in the Participant's Guide.

Bible Study and Daily Bible Readings
Transforming Exercises (Group and Individual)
Teaching Outline

BIBLE STUDY

Read John 13:1-17.

① What is your first impression after reading this story about Jesus' washing his disciples' feet?

② If Jesus' intention was to leave his apprentices with an object lesson, what do you think he wanted them to understand?

③ What would your reaction have been if you have been in the upper room and Jesus began to wash your feet? How does it make you feel right now to think of Jesus serving you?

④ What would it mean in your life if you were to follow Jesus' example in your relationships (at home, at work, at church)?

⑤ Do you know someone who models service in a way that resembles Jesus' way with his disciples? How has he or she been your servant?

Daily Scripture Readings

(from *Study Guide for Celebration of Discipline*, p. 54)

Day	Theme	Passage
Sunday	The call to service	Matthew 20:20-28
Monday	The sign of service	John 13:1-17
Tuesday	The commitment of service	Exodus 21:2, 21:5-6, 1 Corinthians 9:19
Wednesday	The attitude of service	Colossians 3:23-25
Thursday	Service in the Christian fellowship	Romans 12:9-13
Friday	The ministry of small things	Matthew 25:31-39
Saturday	Service exemplified	Luke 10:29-37

SMALL GROUP EXERCISE

Seven Acts of Service

In *Celebration of Discipline* Richard Foster describes seven practical acts of service. Each of these is summarized below. Take a few minutes to reflect on each suggestion and write out how you can perform such an act of service in the coming week. Please be as specific as possible. It may be beneficial to find an accountability partner who will ask you how it went.

1. *The service of guarding the reputation of others*—How can I avoid backbiting and gossip during the coming week?

   _____

   _____

   _____

2. *The service of being served*—How can I avoid the prideful act of refusing to allow myself to be served?

   _____

   _____

   _____

3. *The service of common courtesy*—What deed of compassion can I perform this week?

   _____

   _____

   _____

76   CELEBRATION OF DISCIPLINE

4. *The service of hospitality*—To whom can I offer the generosity of a room, meal, or simple fellowship?

_____

_____

_____

5. *The service of listening*—Who needs my listening ear this week?

_____

_____

_____

6. *The service of bearing the burdens of another*—Do I know a person who is struggling with hurt and suffering? How can I help her or him this week?

_____

_____

_____

7. *The service of sharing the "word of Life" with another. Hearing God for others*—Is there someone I know for whom I strongly believe God would like to whisper a blessing? Can I help by making a time of solitude available, or by providing encouragement from God?

_____

_____

_____

INDIVIDUAL EXERCISES

(See *Celebrating the Disciplines: A Journal Workbook to Accompany Celebration of Discipline*, pp. 43, 44, 150.)

Thoughts

Set aside time for a slow, careful, and meditative reading of the climactic moment recorded in John 13:1-17 (the Bible Study passage for this lesson), when Jesus washed his disciples' feet and then declared of his act of service,

"I have set you an example, that you also should do as I have done to you." (v. 15)

Use the following suggestions to help your reading become an act of intimate fellowship with God:

- Pray that your reading will become a form of communion with God. Imaginatively place yourself in the event, reading the narrative as if you were actually there as one of the disciples.

- Ask God to use key words or phrases to stir an inner response in you. If and when that happens, stop reading and meditate on that word or phrase.

- Pray for insight into what God is teaching you, and for wisdom to apply that insight to your life.

- After reading through the passage at least twice, contemplate its significance as a whole. Then reflect on any particular insights of personal significance to you that emerged while you were reading. Collect and express your thoughts by writing them down.

Emotions

Reflect on what you have experienced as joyous about voluntary service.

Will

Ask God to help you recognize ways in which you are reluctant to submit to others by allowing yourself to be served. Reflect on what this reluctance reveals about your understanding of your relationships with others.

Behavior

Identify an area in which you may be practicing a form of "self-righteous service." Ask God to reveal to you how you may replace it with true service.

Social Interactions

Slow down long enough to practice the service of listening in a context in which you might normally rush past while preoccupied with tasks, time constraints, or your own needs and obligations.

Teaching Outline

BEFORE YOU LEAD: (TIPS FOR FACILITATOR)

I. INTRODUCTION (WELCOME/PRAYER)

II. WARM-UP (OVERVIEW/FREEDOM/DISCUSSION)

III. DVD (VIDEO/TRUTHS/RESPONSE/REFLECTION)

IV. BIBLE STUDY (INSIGHT/EXERCISE/MEDITATION)

V. EXERCISES (GROUP AND INDIVIDUAL)

VI. SUMMARY (RECOMMENDATIONS/RESOURCES)

SESSION TEN:

Confession

BEFORE YOU LEAD

■ Quotes and Quips

Confession draws us into the divine mystery of redemption. At the heart of God is the desire to give and forgive.
Richard J. Foster

A man who confesses his sins in the presence of a brother knows that he is no longer alone with himself; he experiences the presence of God in the reality of the other person.
Dietrich Bonhoeffer

In acts of mutual confession we release the power that heals. Our humanity is no longer denied, but transformed.
Richard J. Foster

Most wonderful of all, confession spells reconciliation with God.
Richard J. Foster

■ Key Scriptures

If we confess our sins, he who is faithful and just will forgive us our sins and cleanse us from all unrighteousness.
1 John 1:9

Confess your sins to one another, and pray for one another, so that you may be healed. The prayer of the righteous is powerful and effective.

James 5:16

■ Note to Leader

If you are using the one-page lesson outlines, you will want to locate that page in the appendix to this lesson or on the CD-ROM now. Please continue to select from the menu of options provided in constructing a lesson tailored to the needs of your group.

■ Materials

For this session *the leader* will need:

- ■ Leader's Guide
- ■ Bible
- ■ DVD Player, Monitor, Stand, Extension Cord, etc.
- ■ *Celebration of Discipline* DVD
- ■ *Celebration of Discipline* (Chapter 10)

For this session *the participant* will need:

- ■ Bible
- ■ Participant's Guide
- ■ Pen or Pencil

SESSION OUTLINE

I. INTRODUCTION
- ■ Welcome
- ■ Prayer

II. WARM-UP
- ■ Overview/Illustration
- ■ Corresponding Freedom
- ■ Discussion of Homework

III. DVD
- ■ Video Vignette
- ■ Central Truths
- ■ Class Response
- ■ Reflection Questions

IV. BIBLE STUDY
- ■ Leader's Insight
- ■ Group Exercise
- ■ Scripture Meditation

V. EXERCISES FOR...
- ■ Small Group Exercise
- ■ Individual Exercises:
  - • Thoughts • Emotions • Will
  - • Behavior • Social Interactions

VI. SUMMARY
- ■ Richard's Recommendations
- ■ Other RENOVARÉ Resources

INTRODUCTION

■ Welcome

Call your group together and welcome the participants to session ten of *Celebration of Discipline*. Our Discipline for this time together is confession.

■ Prayer (See *Prayers From the Heart*, p. 10.)

AN EXAMEN OF CONSCIENCE

"SEARCH ME, O GOD, and know my heart; test me and know my thoughts. See if there is any wicked way in me, and lead me in the way everlasting."

***

God, I pray these words of the psalmist with great hesitation. They are devastatingly honest.
They lay things so bare.
They allow no room for negotiation or compromise.
I fear the scrutiny.
I dread the probe.
I resist the intrusion.

I know that you are all love and so I am entering nothing more than your scrutiny of love. And yet...
No! I refuse to allow my fears to keep me from your love.

***

"Search me, O God, and know my heart; test me and know my thoughts. See if there is any wicked way in me, and lead me in the way everlasting."

Amen.
(The quotation comes from Psalm 139:23, 24.)

WARM-UP

■ Overview and Illustration

What comes to your mind when you think of sin? Breaking a rule—like one of the Ten Commandments? A bad habit—one that seems almost impossible to stop? Images of darkness, chains, or a heavy burden?

Cornelius Plantinga, Jr., in his helpful book *Not the Way It's Supposed to Be: A Breviary of Sin*, has defined sin as the "spoiling of Shalom," or messing up a relationship of peace and intimacy such as Adam and Eve enjoyed with God in the Garden. He argues that once we understand the concept of shalom, we are able to enlarge and clarify our understanding of sin. God, according to Plantinga, hates sin not just because it violates his law, but more substantively "because it breaks the peace and interferes with the way things are supposed to be" (see pp. 14, 15).

The essence of sin is to quit believing that God has our best interests at heart and to shatter the sacred trust that he knows best. The result is a loss of companionship. In sin we move away from his presence, hiding in shame as Adam and Eve did in the Garden. The most diabolical result of sin is a loss of intimate fellowship with God and the loss of peace and tranquility in our relationship with him and others.

The Discipline of confession does so much more than remove the guilt associated with a specific transgression. In confession we come out of hiding and experience a restoration of relationship and shalom. In confession we offer Christ our brokenness and contrition, and he gives to us the key to Eden.

■ Corresponding Freedom

Confession enables us to discover God's desire to give and forgive, and learn more about the nature of God and his desire to live with us in shalom.

■ Homework Check-Up

If your group has decided to read the corresponding chapters of *Celebration of Discipline* and participate in the daily Scripture readings or transforming exercises as outside-of-class activities,

this is the time to do an accountability check and ask for comments concerning the experiences of any participants who would like to share.

DVD

■ Video

In the first segment of this video presentation, Richard Foster provides an introduction to the Discipline of confession. He is assisted through a discussion with Glandion Carney and Margaret Campbell.

If your group desires, you can let the DVD continue through a second segment called "Soul Talk" and listen in on a conversation between Richard and Dallas Willard.

■ Central Truths (pp. 80, 81 in Participant's Guide)

You are provided with a few summary points for the teaching section of each video vignette. Here are the Central Truths for the video session about confession.

- On the cross, just before Jesus committed his spirit to the loving care of the Father, he declared, "It is finished!" But what was finished?

- The usual idea is that people were so bad and God was so angry with us that he had to have somebody take the rap for the whole lot of us, so Jesus had to die on the cross.

- If Jesus' death on the cross *obligates* God to let us into heaven, then he's not forgiving our sins but tolerating our iniquity.

- Any message that gives us a little fire insurance policy without declaring that our lives must be changed and formed into the image of Jesus is not just a half gospel but a false gospel.

- To understand what happened on the cross, we must first realize that it is a great mystery.

- Jesus had observed that three years of teaching the disciples had not brought about real change in their lives. In the Garden of Gethsemane he was wrestling with whether or not his accepting the cross was the only way to accomplish his goal.

■ On the cross Jesus brought into himself all the pain and evil of the entire world—past, present, and future.

■ When Jesus cried out *"Eloi, Eloi, lama sabachthani"* ("My God, my God, why have you forsaken me?"), it was his moment of greatest triumph because he had become so identified with human sin that God had to turn his back.

■ Paul explains in 2 Corinthians 5:21, "For our sake he made him to be sin who knew no sin, so that in him we might become the righteousness of God."

■ What Jesus accomplished on the cross makes confession possible.

■ In confession God heals the sins and sorrows of the past.

■ Class Response

Do you have any questions or observations about the video vignettes before we look at the Reflection Questions together?

■ Reflection Questions (p. 81 in Participant's Guide)

Video: Lecture

① How would you describe the difference between "the toleration of iniquity" and the "forgiveness of sins"?

② How would you explain Richard's understanding of what Jesus meant when he cried out, "It is finished"? How does this relate to the Discipline of confession?

③ In Richard's story about the woman who confessed her sins to him, how would you describe the role he played? How would you describe the role of Christ?

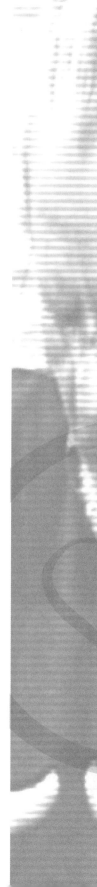

Book (See *Study Guide for Celebration of Discipline*, p. 61.)

1 In your own words, try to describe the theology that lies behind the Discipline of confession.

2 When is the Discipline of confession an unhealthy preoccupation with sin, and when is it a proper recognition of our need for forgiveness?

3 Sometime this week spend fifteen minutes in silence before God and invite him to reveal anything within you that needs to be confessed.

BIBLE STUDY

If time permits, form small groups and allow the participants to complete the Bible study exercise in class.

■ Group Exercise

We will now turn our attention to the Bible as a frame of reference. A brief Bible study can be found on pages 82, 83 in the Participant's Guide and may be used in class or as a homework assignment.

■ Leader's Insight (from *Falling for God*, pp. 183-185)

Consider this: even after a 33-year absence from his true home, Jesus would not return to the joy of heaven until he had reconciled with a fallen friend—the rugged and pigheaded Peter.

Jesus orchestrates a scene that reminds Peter of his initial call into ministry—again, fishing with his friends on the Sea of Galilee. (See Matthew 4:18-21 and John 21:1-20.)

As they return from fishing, having caught nothing all night, Jesus is preparing breakfast for them on the beach. The meal is almost prepared. Jesus shouts to tell them where to locate the fish that had been eluding them all night and then invites them to come and have breakfast. At the sound of Jesus' voice, Peter is in the water like an Olympic swimmer. So desperate is he to be with Jesus that he races the boat to shore.

Participant's Guide p. 82

When the disciples finish eating, Jesus calls Peter aside and asks him three times if he truly loves him—once for each of Peter's rejections 43 days earlier. With each question Jesus was fishing for a confession.

Jesus says, "Simon, son of John, do you truly love me?"

"Truly love" refers to an adoration which involves the entire personality, including the will. It's a love that races up to romantic love and then blows past. It is a love of union—total unity of personality, including the will, with Jesus.

Peter replies that he "loves" Jesus. But the word he uses implies a simple brotherly love or fondness.

If your spouse asked you if you were head-over-heels, wholeheartedly in love with her (or him)—so much that you have no will apart from his or her own, would you dare to reply, "Yes, dear. You know I'm fond of you"?

No, of course not!

And Jesus, as part of the restoration of Peter and his invitation to restored relationship, wants him to feel the difference between these two types of "love."

Maybe Peter was still feeling sheepish after his bitterly painful denial of Christ. Maybe he can hardly imagine that Jesus is inviting him to a deep love relationship.

But that is Jesus' invitation to Peter. And I dare say that Jesus has been asking the same question for almost 2,000 years. He's asking you and me right now, "Are you head-over-heels in love with me? Will you live your life so close to me that our wills are united and our hearts beat as one?"

Peter's sins were not overlooked. Jesus' three questions were pointed reminders of Peter's three denials. But the specific sins were not the point. Jesus' invitation was to a restoration of the spoiled shalom. The goal of confession is always reconciliation and restored relationship.

■ Scripture Meditation

Please note that the Bible Study also includes suggestions for daily Scripture readings (p. 83 in Participant's Guide). Encourage the group participants to spend five to ten minutes with these passages of Scripture each day. As you progress through these sessions, the participants may want to expand this time frame and use these daily passages as part of *lectio divina*.

TRANSFORMING EXERCISES

Please see pages 84-87 in the Participant's Guide to observe the suggested *Small Group Exercise* and *Individual Exercises*. The *Small Group Exercise* is typically designed for use during your session together. The *Individual Exercises* are based on Dallas Willard's five components of the person and are constructed for the participants to use as homework activities.

SMALL GROUP

Participant's Guide p. 84

INDIVIDUAL

Participant's Guide p. 86

SUMMARY

■ Review

As Richard reminds us in his tender reframing of Jesus' death, it was love and not anger that brought him to the cross: "Golgotha came as a result of God's great desire to forgive" (*Celebration of Discipline*, p. 143). While sin may correctly be seen as specific acts of transgression, it is most helpfully viewed as breaking the sacred trust that God has our best interests at heart and moving away from relationship with him. Sin is the shattering of shalom, and as such, it is an offense to the love of God. While confession involves contrition over specific offenses, it looks beyond them to the joy of coming back home to God.

■ Richard's Recommendations

Something old: *The Confessions of St. Augustine,* 354-430, translated by William C. Creasy. (Notre Dame, IN: Ave Maria Press, 2003)

Something new: *The Healing Light* by Agnes Sanford. (New York: Ballentine Books, 1983, pp. 111-117)

■ Other RENOVARÉ Resources

"The Prayer of Confession" from *The Book of Common Prayer* (New York: Church Hymnal Corporation, 1979), p. 360.

APPENDIX

Use the appendix that follows to facilitate class exercises and homework. The *Bible Study, Small Group Exercise*, and *Individual Exercises* can be found in the Participant's Guide.

Bible Study and Daily Bible Readings
Transforming Exercises (Group and Individual)
Teaching Outline

BIBLE STUDY

Read John 21:1-19.

① Three times Peter had denied he even knew Jesus—what sin could be worse than that? Peter was in agony. In this story we observe Peter with Jesus after the Resurrection. If you had been Peter, what would you feel when Jesus called?

② What is the most amazing aspect of this story for you?

③ What seems to be Jesus' number one goal?

④ How does this story give you hope for restoration of relationship with Jesus after you sin (break the shalom)?

⑤ What words best describe your relationship with God, fondness or head-over-heels in love?

Daily Scripture Readings

(from *Study Guide for Celebration of Discipline*, p. 60)

Day	Theme	Passage
Sunday	The need for confession and forgiveness	Isaiah 59:1-9, Romans 3:10-18
Monday	The promise of forgiveness	Jeremiah 31:34, Matthew 26:28, Ephesians 1:7
Tuesday	The assurance of forgiveness	1 John 1:5-10
Wednesday	Jesus Christ, our Adequate Savior, Mediator, and Advocate	2 Timothy 1:8-10, 1 Timothy 2:5, 1 John 2:1
Thursday	A parable of confession	Luke 15:11-24
Friday	Authority and forgiveness	Matthew 16:19, 18:18, John 20:23
Saturday	The ministry of the Christian Fellowship	James 5:13-16

S M A L L   G R O U P   E X E R C I S E

Giving a Confession

In *Celebration of Discipline* Richard Foster gives suggestions for how we should offer a confession. These suggestions will be summarized below. We recommend that you take a few minutes to react to each suggestion in silent conversation with God, and then use them to prepare yourself for the prayer of confession found in *The Book of Common Prayer.* (Note: Your leader may have you do this in preparation for viewing the video session and participating in the group exercise, or you may use this exercise as an additional small group experience or part of your private devotions.)

Four Things Necessary for Giving a Good Confession

(Please see *Celebration of Discipline,* pp. 151-153, for a more detailed exposition of the suggestions by St. Alphonsus Liguori.)

① An examination of conscience

Here "we are inviting God to move upon the heart and show us areas that need his forgiving and healing touch."

② Sorrow

Sorrow "is an abhorrence of having committed the sin, a deep regret at having offended the heart of the Father.... [It] is a way of taking the confession seriously."

③ Determination to avoid sin

Determination "is the *will* to be delivered from sin that we seek from God as we prepare to make confession."

④ **A definite termination point**

"There must be a definite termination point in the self-examination process. Otherwise, we can easily fall into a permanent habit of self-condemnation. Confession begins in sorrow, but it ends in joy."

A Classic Prayer of Confession

Most merciful God, we confess that we have sinned against you in thought, word, and deed, by what we have done, and by what we have left undone. We have not loved you with our whole heart; we have not loved our neighbors as ourselves. We are truly sorry and we humbly repent. For the sake of your Son Jesus Christ, have mercy on us and forgive us; that we may delight in your will, and walk in your ways, to the glory of your Name. *Amen.*

INDIVIDUAL EXERCISES

(See *Celebrating the Disciplines: A Journal Workbook to Accompany Celebration of Discipline*, pp. 50, 51.)

Thoughts

Memorize 1 John 1:9. "If we confess our sins, he who is faithful and just will forgive us our sins and cleanse us from all unrighteousness."

Emotions

Let any feelings of guilt over past transgressions—which you have already confessed to God—be an occasion to remind the Thief and Robber of the promise contained in 1 John 1:9.

Will

During a session of prayer and meditation, seek the Spirit's prompting for any confession God wants you to make—whether to God alone, to a trusted individual, or to a group to which you belong. In preparation for confession, ask yourself these questions:

- "What specific sins do I need to become aware of under the gaze of God?"

- "Am I willing to experience godly sorrow for my sin?"

- "Do I truly yearn to live a holy life?"

- "Do I understand, and am I able to accept, the forgiveness God extends to me?"

Behavior

Ask God to make you aware of any opportunity this week to radiate the light of Christ by receiving another person's confession—in whatever form that unburdening of sin may take. If the opportunity arises, pray for spiritual sensitivity in these areas: listening carefully and quietly; praying inwardly, in the light of the cross, that the other person will receive Christ's love and forgiveness through you; proclaiming personally the powerful reality of Christ's forgiveness for another; praying aloud with him or her for healing the inner wounds of sin; keeping private information private; and responding to how God is ministering to you through this experience.

Social Interactions

Reflect on Jesus' desire to forgive and restore Peter (see Bible Study). Consider how marvelous it is for the Creator of the universe to long for reconciliation and a return to shalom. Allow this amazing reality to motivate you to offer reconciliation to those who have sinned against you.

Teaching Outline

BEFORE YOU LEAD: (TIPS FOR FACILITATOR)

I. INTRODUCTION (WELCOME/PRAYER)

II. WARM-UP (OVERVIEW/FREEDOM/DISCUSSION)

III. DVD (VIDEO/TRUTHS/RESPONSE/REFLECTION)

IV. BIBLE STUDY (INSIGHT/EXERCISE/MEDITATION)

V. EXERCISES (GROUP AND INDIVIDUAL)

VI. SUMMARY (RECOMMENDATIONS/RESOURCES)

Notes

_____

_____

_____

_____

_____

_____

_____

_____

_____

_____

_____

_____

_____

_____

_____

_____

_____

_____

Worship

BEFORE YOU LEAD

■ Quotes and Quips

Worship is our response to the overtures of love from the heart of the Father....It is kindled within us only when the Spirit of God touches our human spirit.

Richard J. Foster

[Worship] is celestial manna falling from the sky, pouring down grace; it is the holy kingdom in the soul, it is the bread of angels consumed on earth as it is in heaven.

Jean-Pierre de Caussade

The heart and soul of worship is the confession that Jesus Christ is alive and well among us and here to teach his people himself....When we experience him among us, worship comes alive.

Richard J. Foster

■ Key Scriptures

Worship the Lord in holy splendor; tremble before him, all the earth.

Psalm 96:9

...My soul magnifies the Lord, and my spirit rejoices in God my Savior.

Luke 1:46, 47

Since we are receiving a kingdom that cannot be shaken, let us give thanks, by which we offer to God an acceptable worship with reverence and awe.

Hebrews 12:28

■ Note to Leader

If you are using the one-page lesson outlines, you will want to locate that page in the appendix to this lesson or on the CD-ROM now. Please continue to select from the menu of options provided in constructing a lesson tailored to the needs of your group.

■ Materials

For this session *the leader* will need:

- Leader's Guide
- Bible
- DVD Player, Monitor, Stand, Extension Cord, etc.
- *Celebration of Discipline* DVD
- *Celebration of Discipline* (Chapter 11)

For this session *the participant* will need:

- Bible
- Participant's Guide
- Pen or Pencil

SESSION OUTLINE

I. INTRODUCTION
- Welcome
- Prayer

II. WARM-UP
- Overview/Illustration
- Corresponding Freedom
- Discussion of Homework

III. DVD
- Video Vignette
- Central Truths
- Class Response
- Reflection Questions

IV. BIBLE STUDY
- Leader's Insight
- Group Exercise
- Scripture Meditation

V. EXERCISES FOR...
- Small Group Exercise
- Individual Exercises:
  - Thoughts • Emotions • Will
  - Behavior • Social Interactions

VI. SUMMARY
- Richard's Recommendations
- Other RENOVARÉ Resources

INTRODUCTION

■ Welcome

Call your group together and welcome the participants to session eleven of *Celebration of Discipline*. Our Discipline for this time together is worship.

■ Prayer (See *Prayers From the Heart*, p. 70.)

A PRAYER OF ECSTASY

FIRE
God of Abraham, God of Isaac, God of Jacob,
not of the philosophers and scholars.
Certitude.
> *Certitude.*
>> *Feeling.*
>>> *Joy.*
>>>> *Peace.*
God of Jesus Christ.
Forgetfulness of the world and everything, except God.
Greatness of the Human Soul.
Joy, joy, joy, tears of joy.

Blaise Pascal

WARM-UP

■ Overview and Illustration

Richard Foster begins both his chapter on worship and the video vignette with the following quote from Archbishop William Temple:

> *To worship is to quicken the **conscience** by the holiness of God, to feed the **mind** with the truth of God, to purge the **imagination** by the beauty of God, to open the **heart** to the love of God, to devote the **will** to the purpose of God.* (emphasis added)

What seems most striking about Temple's beautiful description is the way he captures the holistic nature of worship. In worship a person becomes keenly aware of the presence of the resurrected Christ (*Celebration of Discipline*, p. 158) and responds to his overtures of love. In worship the heart of God touches the human heart and affects every aspect of the person.

The following diagram contains Dallas Willard's model of the person and also provides an excellent visual illustration of what happens in worship. The awareness of and receptivity to the real presence of Christ touches each component of the person as the heart is opened to his transforming presence, and communion begins. In a sense, the experience of worship is a microcosm of the process of

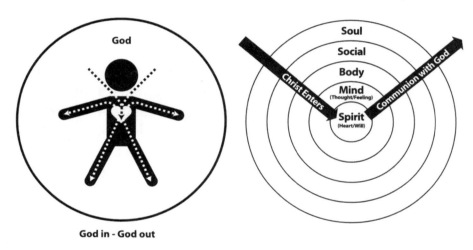

Christian formation.

To echo the language of William Temple, when the spirit of worship falls on us, we are touched by the holiness of God, hear the truth of God, experience the beauty of God, enter into the love of God, and begin to be made one with the will of God.

A Word of Humility

But special care must be taken, or the beauty of worship experience can become the bane of worship practice. Humans are finite; we exist in a very limited number of aspects (thought, feeling, will, behavior, relationship). And as long as we are finite, we must have forms, or liturgical expressions, for worship. As Richard says in the video vignette, while we do have a choice of liturgy, we do not have a choice whether or not to use liturgy.

What does this mean in practical terms? As finite human

beings, we often show a tendency to "specialize" in or "favor" one or more of our components as we experience God. For some of us, our thought life tends to dominate. Consequently, well-crafted sermons may be the most important aspect of our worship liturgy. For others, feeling and experience prevail and lead to greater emphasis on music or dramatic presentations in worship. Others may place special importance on how the body becomes part of worship practices (whether by kneeling quietly or by dancing and clapping loudly). And some give prominence to the confession of a surrendered will, or how worship should result in energy for social justice.

But true worship is the holistic expression of Heart touching heart, affecting the whole person. While for any finite human being, the expression may seem keenest in one aspect of our personhood, we must resist the temptation to believe that our way is "best."

God's generous gift of worship calls for a ceasefire in all "worship wars" and a recognition that it is not liturgical expression that is important, but the experience of God in our midst. In Richard's words, "What we are committed to is reality—real worship, real confession, real praise, real adoration. If particular forms at particular times bring us more fully into worship, we are free to use them; if not, too bad for the forms. We are free to use the highest liturgy, no form at all, or anything in between so long as it brings us into real worship. The forms of worship must always be subject to the reality of worship." (*Study Guide for Celebration of Discipline*, p. 63)

■ Corresponding Freedom

Worship frees us for the experience of reality—the experience of God.

■ Homework Check-Up

If your group has decided to read the corresponding chapters of *Celebration of Discipline* and participate in the daily Scripture readings or transforming exercises as outside-of-class activities, this is the time to do an accountability check and ask for comments concerning the experiences of any participants who would like to share.

DVD

■ Video

In the first segment of this video presentation, Richard Foster offers a brief overview of worship before requesting that George Skramstad provide a musical history of Christian worship.

If your group desires, you can let the DVD continue through a second segment called "Soul Talk" and listen in on a conversation between Richard and Dallas Willard.

■ Central Truths (pp. 88, 89 in Participant's Guide)

There are only a few summary points for this lesson. The majority of the video vignette is devoted to George Skramstad's musical history of worship.

■ In true worship each component of the person is involved and affected.

■ Worship is the greatest thing that human beings can do. It ushers us into the holy of holies, where we are enabled to see the Lord high and lifted up. It catches us up into a high, holy adventure.

■ There are two major contexts for worship:
 ◆ The Context of Common Life
  • Consider Paul's words in 1 Corinthians 10:31: "Whether you eat or drink, or whatever you do, do everything for the glory of God."
 ◆ The Specifically Religious Context
  • In the specifically religious context we utilize liturgies of worship. There are no nonliturgical Christians. While we have a choice about what type of liturgy we will use in worship, we do not have a choice not to use liturgy.
  • A verse that supports this idea is 2 Corinthians 4:7: "We have this treasure in clay jars, so that it may be made clear that this extraordinary power belongs to God and does not come from us."
  • The treasure to which Paul was referring is the glory of God in the face of Jesus Christ. The vessel is the

human body and the cultural forms with which we enshroud the treasure.

■ One of the finest "vessels" for worship that we have is music. Music is one of the most important liturgical expressions.

■ George Skramstad provides a little tour of the history of worship music.

■ Class Response

Do you have any questions or observations about the video vignettes before we look at the Reflection Questions together?

■ Reflection Questions (p. 89 in Participant's Guide)

Video: Lecture

1 What do you think of William Temple's "holistic" definition of worship?

2 Which context for worship—common life or religious context—seems most natural for you? What are your ideas for further developing both contexts for worship in your life?

3 What is your reaction to the history of worship music presented by George Skramstad?

Book (See *Study Guide for Celebration of Discipline*, pp. 65, 66.)

1 How can we cultivate "holy expectancy"?

2 Which forms of worship you have experienced have been especially meaningful to you? Do you have any sense of why these particular forms have been more meaningful than others?

3 Critique the rather bold statement that the Bible does not bind us to any form (that is, wineskin) of worship. Can you think of any worship forms that should be universally binding upon all cultures of Christians at all times?

[Richard Foster writes], "Just as worship begins in Holy Expectancy it ends in Holy Obedience." What does that mean for you this next week?

BIBLE STUDY

If time permits, form small groups and allow the participants to complete the Bible study exercise in class.

■ Group Exercise

We will now turn our attention to the Bible as a frame of reference. A brief Bible study can be found on page 90 in the Participant's Guide and may be used in class or as a homework assignment.

■ Leader's Insight

Worship is the experience of the risen Lord in our midst. Worship is the reality of Immanuel—God with us.

At the heart of the RENOVARÉ *Spiritual Formation Bible* is the overarching theme of Scripture: God's desire to be *with us*, the "Immanuel principle." As Richard Foster says in its introduction, "The unity of the Bible is discovered in the development of life 'with God' as a reality on earth, centered in the person of Jesus. We might call this *The Immanuel Principle* of life."

The verses selected for the Bible Study for this lesson provide an overview of God's desire to be with us.

Participant's Guide p. 90

Genesis 1:26-28, 3:8	Adam and Eve were created to live in partnership with God, encountering Him face-to-face.
Exodus 25:8, 9	After the Fall, God gives the people the Mosaic Law, the Ark of the Covenant and the Tabernacle as a reminder of his presence in their midst.

1 Kings 8:10-13	The temple was built as a more permanent place for God to dwell with his people.
Luke 17:20, 21	The most central teaching theme for the ministry of Jesus is that "the kingdom of God is among you."
John 16:5-7	Jesus promises his disciples that he will send "the Counselor" (the Holy Spirit) to be with them in his place.
Acts 2:1-4.	The Holy Spirit comes at Pentecost

Worship captures the greatest theme of Scripture. To worship is to experience the reality of God in our midst, a God who desires to be *with* his people in joyous celebration of life.

■ Scripture Meditation

Please note that the Bible Study also includes suggestions for daily Scripture readings (p. 90 in Participant's Guide). Encourage the group participants to spend five to ten minutes with these passages of Scripture each day. As you progress through these sessions, the participants may want to expand this time frame and use these daily passages as part of *lectio divina*.

TRANSFORMING EXERCISES

Please see pages 91-93 in the Participant's Guide to observe the suggested *Small Group Exercise* and *Individual Exercises*. The *Small Group Exercise* is typically designed for use during your session together. The *Individual Exercises* are based on Dallas Willard's five components of the person and are constructed for the participants to use as homework activities.

SMALL GROUP

Participant's Guide p. 91

INDIVIDUAL

Participant's Guide p. 93

SUMMARY

■ Review

Worship is the expression in words, music, rituals, and silent adoration of the greatness, beauty, and goodness of God, by means of which we enter the supranatural reality of the *shekinah*, or glory of God (from the Spiritual Disciplines Index of *The RENOVARÉ Spiritual Formation Bible*). Worship is a transforming celebration of God that is expressed through both a variety of liturgical styles in a religious context, and in the context of common life as we learn to do all things to the glory of God.

■ Richard's Recommendations

Something old: *Worship* by Evelyn Underhill, 1875-1941. (Eugene, OR: Wipf & Stock, 2002)

Something new: *Reaching Out Without Dumbing Down* by Marva Dawn. (Grand Rapids, MI: Eerdmans, 1995)

■ Other RENOVARÉ Resources

Songs for Renewal by Janet Lindeblad Janzen with Richard J. Foster. (San Francisco: HarperSanFrancisco, 1995)

APPENDIX

Use the appendix that follows to facilitate class exercises and homework. The *Bible Study, Small Group Exercise*, and *Individual Exercises* can be found in the Participant's Guide.

Bible Study and Daily Bible Readings
Transforming Exercises (Group and Individual)
Teaching Outline

BIBLE STUDY

Read Genesis 1:26-28, 3:8; Exodus 25:8, 9; 1 Kings 8:10-13; Luke 17:20, 21; John 16:5-7; and Acts 2:1-4.

1 How does each of these passages illustrate the "Immanuel Principle," God's desire to be *with* his people?

2 After Adam and Eve were disobedient, what they did next was almost as bad as their sin: they hid from God. Are you aware of a pattern of hiding from God in your own life? What do you believe is a better solution than withdrawing from God's presence?

3 How do you experience the notion of God's desiring to be *with* you, in ongoing conversation and communion?

4 How does worship relate to the *"with God"* theme that can be traced throughout Scripture?

Daily Scripture Readings

(from *Study Guide for Celebration of Discipline*, p. 65)

Day	Theme	Passage
Sunday	Worship in spirit and truth	John 4:19-24
Monday	Communion: the essence of worship	John 6:52-58, 6:63
Tuesday	The life of worship	Ephesians 5:18-20, Colossians 3:16-17
Wednesday	The Lord high and lifted up	Isaiah 6:1-8
Thursday	Sing to the Lord	Psalm 96
Friday	Worship of all creation	Psalm 148
Saturday	Worthy is the Lamb	Revelation 5:6-14

SESSION ELEVEN

SMALL GROUP EXERCISE

Wonder and Worship in the Common Life

Richard Foster reminds us that worship occurs in two contexts: in addition to a specifically religious framework, worship can arise from within the context of common life. God's beauty expressed in his creation is a sometimes overlooked venue for worship. Take some time to reflect on the following prayer (either by pondering silently or listening as someone slowly reads the lines), and then make a commitment to set aside some time for experiencing the wonder of God as expressed in nature.

A PRAYER OF WONDER (See *Prayers From the Heart*, p. 66.)

I GLORY in your handiwork, O God:
    towering mountains and deep valleys,
    dense forests and expansive deserts,
    fathomless depths of blue below and immeasurable
    heights of blue above.

When I peer into the universe of the telescope
and the universe of the microscope I stand in awe at:
    the complexity and the simplicity,
    the order and the chaos,
    and the infinite variety of colors everywhere.

When I watch the little creatures that creep upon the earth
I marvel at:
    such purpose,
      such direction,
        such design;

and yet
> such freedom,
>> such openness,
>>> such creativity.

O Lord God, Creator of the hummingbird and the
Milky Way, I am lost in wonder at your originality.
Amen.

ACTIVITY

(See *Spiritual Classics,* pp. 264-270.)

Take a nature walk this week. Give yourself enough time so that you
will not be hurried or rushed. Relax and experience the splendor of God's
creation wherever you discover it: in a sunrise, in light splintering across
water, in an unfolding bud or a massive tree. Dwell in the experience and
be grateful for it.

INDIVIDUAL EXERCISES

(See *Celebration of Discipline*, pp. 170-173, and *Celebrating the Disciplines: A Journal Workbook to Accompany Celebration of Discipline*, p. 55.)

Thoughts

A. W. Tozer says, "The essence of idolatry is the entertainment of thoughts about God that are unworthy of Him" (quoted in *Celebration of Discipline*, p. 159). Richard Foster amplifies this statement with the observation that "To think rightly about God is to have everything right. To think wrongly about God, in an important sense, is to have everything wrong." Ask God to reveal to you any wrong images of him in your mind (e.g., God as a cosmic sheriff or a senile grandfather or a productivity monitor). Then ask that he begin to erase these images as he paints more accurate pictures in your mind.

Emotions

Cultivate holy dependency. Holy dependency means you are utterly and completely dependent upon God for anything significant to happen. Guard against any feelings of self-sufficiency as you go through the week. Notice and learn from the emotions associated with your experience of holy dependency.

Will

Learn to practice the presence of God daily. Really try to follow Paul's words, "Pray without ceasing" (1 Thessalonians 5:17, KJV). Punctuate every moment with inward whisperings of adoration, praise, and thanksgiving.

Behavior

Practice a "perpetual, inward, listening silence" this week in preparation for corporate worship.

Social Interactions

In your next meeting with other believers, practice a "holy expectancy" in preparation for your worship together. How does it affect your participation in worship?

Teaching Outline

BEFORE YOU LEAD: (TIPS FOR FACILITATOR)

I. INTRODUCTION (WELCOME/PRAYER)

II. WARM-UP (OVERVIEW/FREEDOM/DISCUSSION)

III. DVD (VIDEO/TRUTHS/RESPONSE/REFLECTION)

IV. BIBLE STUDY (INSIGHT/EXERCISE/MEDITATION)

V. EXERCISES (GROUP AND INDIVIDUAL)

VI. SUMMARY (RECOMMENDATIONS/RESOURCES)

Notes

SESSION TWELVE:
Guidance

BEFORE YOU LEAD

■ Quotes and Quips

The will of God is discovered as we become acquainted with God, learn His ways, and become His friend. …As the friendship grows…we will know instinctively what actions would please Him, what decisions would be in accord with His way.

Richard J. Foster

Dwell in the life and love and power and wisdom of God, in unity one with another and with God. And the peace and wisdom of God fill all your hearts so that nothing may rule in you but the life, which stands in the Lord God.

George Fox

God has created us for intimate friendship with himself— both now and forever. Jesus came to earth to respond to the universal human need to know how to live well.

Dallas Willard

■ Key Scriptures

In your steadfast love you led the people whom you redeemed; you guided them by your strength to your holy abode.

Exodus 15:13

When the Spirit of truth comes, he will guide you into all the truth....

John 16:13

If we live by the Spirit, let us also be guided by the Spirit.

Galatians 5:25

■ Note to Leader

If you are using the one-page lesson outlines, you will want to locate that page in the appendix to this lesson or on the CD-ROM now. Please continue to select from the menu of options provided in constructing a lesson tailored to the needs of your group.

■ Materials

For this session *the leader* will need:

- Leader's Guide
- Bible
- DVD Player, Monitor, Stand, Extension Cord, etc.
- *Celebration of Discipline* DVD
- *Celebration of Discipline* (Chapter 12)

For this session *the participant* will need:

- Bible
- Participant's Guide
- Pen or Pencil

SESSION OUTLINE

I. INTRODUCTION
- ■ Welcome
- ■ Prayer

II. WARM-UP
- ■ Overview/Illustration
- ■ Corresponding Freedom
- ■ Discussion of Homework

III. DVD
- ■ Video Vignette
- ■ Central Truths
- ■ Class Response
- ■ Reflection Questions

IV. BIBLE STUDY
- ■ Leader's Insight
- ■ Group Exercise
- ■ Scripture Meditation

V. EXERCISES FOR...
- ■ Small Group Exercise
- ■ Individual Exercises:
  - • Thoughts • Emotions • Will
  - • Behavior • Social Interactions

VI. SUMMARY
- ■ Richard's Recommendations
- ■ Other RENOVARÉ Resources

INTRODUCTION

■ Welcome

Call your group together and welcome the participants to session twelve of *Celebration of Discipline*. Our Discipline for this time together is guidance.

■ Prayer (See *Prayers From the Heart*, p. 41.)

SPEAK, LORD, FOR YOUR SERVANT IS LISTENING

Speak, Lord, for your servant is listening. Incline my heart to your words, and let your speech come upon me as dew upon the grass.

In days gone by the children of Israel said to Moses, "Speak to us and we shall listen; do not let the Lord speak to us, lest we die." This is not how I pray, Lord. No. With the great prophet Samuel, I humbly and earnestly beg: "Speak, Lord, for your servant is listening."

So, do not let Moses speak to me, but you, O Lord, my God, eternal Truth, you speak to me.

If I hear your voice, may I not be condemned
for hearing the word and not following it,
for knowing it and not loving it,
for believing it and not living it.
Speak then, Lord, for your servant listens, for you have the words of eternal life. Speak to me to comfort my soul and to change my whole life: in turn, may it give you praise and glory and honor, forever and ever.

Amen.

Thomas à Kempis

WARM-UP

■ Overview and Illustration

Have you heard the quote, "If you want to hear the flutes, you'd better sit on the front row"? It's pretty good advice—and not just for listening to an orchestra.

When it comes to practical discernment—obtaining guidance from God—the most important thing is to organize our lives in such a way that we are keeping close company with Jesus. We hear Christ best by becoming his friend and spending lots of time with him.

Dallas Willard expressed it this way in *Hearing God: Developing a Conversational Relationship With God*:

> Our union with God—his presence with us, in which our aloneness is banished and the meaning and full purpose of human existence [are] realized—*consists chiefly in [developing] a conversational relationship with God while we are each consistently and deeply engaged as his friend and co-laborer in the affairs of the kingdom of the heavens.*

The goal of guidance is not specific instructions about how to "get information from God." Guidance is not a matter of letting our Bible flop open to reveal God's opinion on a matter, or even asking our pastor what to do in a specific situation. Guidance comes from developing a conversational relationship with God, and its ultimate end is an issue of conformity to the image of Christ.

Okay, you may be thinking, *I get it. The first, second, and third steps toward guidance are about becoming Jesus' friend, staying close so we can hear. But what about when I have a very specific question and I can't tell if I've heard God's voice or my own thoughts? And why is guidance listed as a corporate Discipline?*

In the video vignette, Richard Foster tells the story about a harbor off the coast of Italy that is so treacherous three lighthouses had to be built for directing ships. The only way to know if you are in the safe passageway is to follow a course in which you see all three lights as one. If the beacons are not perfectly aligned and you see two or all three lights, you are off course.

Richard then suggests that we are most sure we have received guidance from God when our personal perception of his voice is in line with other normal means of guidance, such as the whole tenor

of Scripture, advice from the Christian community (ranging from spiritual direction to group meetings for clearness of discernment), and Divine providence (God making circumstances work for his will).

Individual guidance, while of immense importance, must in the end yield to verification from corporate guidance. The leading of the Spirit is always to be in concert with God's Spirit-empowered community. It is in that symphony of voices that the melodious tone of God is most clearly heard.

■ Corresponding Freedom

Through God's guidance we become a Spirit-led, Spirit-intoxicated, Spirit-empowered people.

■ Homework Check-Up

If your group has decided to read the corresponding chapters of *Celebration of Discipline* and participate in the daily Scripture readings or transforming exercises as outside-of-class activities, this is the time to do an accountability check and ask for comments concerning the experiences of any participants who would like to share.

DVD

■ Video

In the first segment of this video presentation, Richard Foster provides an introduction to the Discipline of guidance. He is assisted through a discussion with Glandion Carney and Margaret Campbell.

If your group desires, you can let the DVD continue through a second segment called "Soul Talk" and listen in on a conversation between Richard and Dallas Willard.

■ Central Truths (pp. 94, 95 in Participant's Guide)

You are provided with a few summary points for the teaching section of each video vignette. Here are the Central Truths for the video session about guidance.

■ Heaven and earth are on tiptoe waiting for the emergence of a Spirit-led, Spirit-intoxicated, Spirit-empowered people.

■ But such a people will not emerge until there is among us a deeper, more profound experience of an Immanuel of the Spirit—*God with us*.

■ The Discipline of guidance teaches us to become the friend of God and to learn and discern the voice of the true Shepherd.

■ It takes some practice to learn to know the voice of God, the *Kol Yahweh*.

■ The fact that God speaks to us is no guarantee that we hear correctly.

■ There are some important parallels between learning to recognize God's voice and learning to distinguish a human voice. Three things about a human voice help us know who is speaking:
   ◆ The **tone** of the voice—
      • God does not push and condemn; he draws and encourages.
   ◆ The **quality** of the voice—
      • The voice of God will be like that of Jesus: gentle and merciful.
   ◆ The **content** of the voice—
      • God will speak in a way that is consistent with how he has spoken in the past.

■ There are two broad categories or means of guidance: normal and exceptional.
   ◆ The **normal** means of guidance are
      • Scripture
      • Direct revelation
      • Divine providence
      • The Christian community
      • Personal integrity
   ◆ The **exceptional** means of guidance are
      • Fleeces
      • Angels
      • Dreams
      • Visions
      • Signs

■ It is important to understand that exceptional means of guidance are not necessarily compliments—they may mean we are hard of hearing.

■ The means of guidance work together; one by itself is dangerous.

■ Class Response

Do you have any questions or observations about the video vignettes before we look at the Reflection Questions together?

■ Reflection Questions (p. 95 in Participant's Guide)

Video: Lecture

1 How do you experience the Immanuel ("with-God") principle in your life?

2 What are some things you do that help you develop a friendship with God?

3 Have you had an experience in which listening for the tone, quality, or content of God's voice has been helpful to your own process of practical discernment?

Book (See *Study Guide for Celebration of Discipline*, pp. 69, 70.)

1 Is the idea of guidance as a *corporate Discipline* new or strange to you?

2 What do you understand the idea of a "spiritual director" to mean? Are there dangers to the idea? Are there advantages to the idea?

3 Do you think that the notion of a people under the direct theocratic rule of God is workable, or is it only an illusory pipe dream? (Question 3 not in Participant's Guide)

BIBLE STUDY

If time permits, form small groups and allow the participants to complete the Bible study exercise in class.

■ Group Exercise

We will now turn our attention to the Bible as a frame of reference. A brief Bible study can be found on pages 96, 97 in the Participant's Guide and may be used in class or as a homework assignment.

■ Leader's Insight

According to Dallas Willard (in *Hearing God*, p. 33), "We demean God immeasurably by casting him in the role of the cosmic boss, foreman or autocrat, whose chief joy in relation to humans is ordering them around, taking pleasure in seeing them jump at his command and painstakingly noting down any failures." Such images can haunt the imaginations of those desiring to see and hear God clearly. Most false images of God can send us into hiding instead of moving us toward God in love and expectation.

Instead of the common but false picture of God as a stern and impersonal boss, we are to see him as our friend—see 2 Chronicles 20:7 and John 15:12-15. The role of taskmaster, whether a pleased one or an angry one, is a role that God accepts only when appointed to it by our own limited understanding (*Hearing God*, p. 33).

To be God's friend means that we are keeping his commandments (John 15:14)—the greatest of which is to love him with our whole person and our neighbors as ourselves. To be God's buddy (in addition to being his servant) means that we are welcomed into a close and intimate relationship. As friends, we are taken into God's confidence; we are able to understand his plans and purposes because we are staying as close to him as branches to a vine. From this intimate perspective, guidance is relatively easy. Two wills are becoming one.

BIBLE STUDY

Participant's Guide p. 96

■ Scripture Meditation

Please note that the Bible Study also includes suggestions for daily Scripture readings (p. 97 in Participant's Guide). Encourage the group participants to spend five to ten minutes with these passages of Scripture each day. As you progress through these sessions, the participants may want to expand this time frame and use these daily passages as part of *lectio divina*.

TRANSFORMING EXERCISES

Please see pages 98-101 in the Participant's Guide to observe the suggested *Small Group Exercise* and *Individual Exercises*. The *Small Group Exercise* is typically designed for use during your session together. The *Individual Exercises* are based on Dallas Willard's five components of the person and are constructed for the participants to use as homework activities.

SUMMARY

■ Review

Richard Foster begins Chapter 12 of his *Study Guide for Celebration of Discipline* with these words: "Guidance is the most radical of the Disciplines because it goes to the heart of this matter of walking with God. Guidance means the glorious life of hearing God's voice and obeying His word" (p. 68).

Perhaps those words sound familiar. We learned in session two that the Discipline of meditation involves learning to hear and obey the *Kol Yahweh*, the voice of God. And this is exactly right. Both Disciplines (indeed, all of the Disciplines) have the goal of being with God for the purpose of conformity to the image of Christ.

By contrast, guidance is listed as a corporate Discipline because more is needed than individual listening. Personal direction from God must yield to and harmonize with corporate guidance. It is best when we are led by the Spirit *together*.

SMALL GROUP

Participant's Guide p. 98

INDIVIDUAL

Participant's Guide p. 100

◼ Richard's Recommendations

Something old: *The Imitation of Christ* by Thomas à Kempis, ca. 1379-1471. (Notre Dame, IN: Ave Maria, 2003).

Something new: *Hearing God* by Dallas Willard. (Downers Grove, IL: Varsity, 1999).

◼ Other RENOVARÉ Resources

Spiritual Classics edited by Emilie Griffin and Richard J. Foster. (San Francisco, HarperSanFrancisco, 1999, pp. 277-306)

APPENDIX

Use the appendix that follows to facilitate class exercises and homework. The *Bible Study, Small Group Exercise*, and *Individual Exercises* can be found in the Participant's Guide.

Bible Study and Daily Bible Readings
Transforming Exercises (Group and Individual)
Teaching Outline

BIBLE STUDY

Read 2 Chronicles 20:7 and John 15:12-15.

1   In 2 Chronicles 20:7, the writer refers to Abraham as God's "friend." Does this description surprise you? What do you think it means to say that Abraham was God's friend?

2   In the passage from John, Jesus says that he calls his disciples no longer servants but friends. Do you feel more like Jesus' servant or his friend? What are some ways you can go about developing a friendship with Jesus?

3   How would you explain the difference between being someone's servant and being his friend?

4   In the same passage, Jesus says we are his friends if we do what he commands. If you had to pick the most important commandment of Jesus, what would you say? (Hint: John 15:12 seems to contain the answer.)

Daily Scripture Readings

(from *Study Guide for Celebration of Discipline*, p. 69)

Day	Theme	Passage
Sunday	The polestar of faith	Hebrews 11
Monday	The guidance of divine Providence	Genesis 24:1-21
Tuesday	The guidance of justice and obedience	Isaiah 1:17, 18-20
Wednesday	Led into all truth	Proverbs 3:5-6, John 14:6, 16:13, Acts 10:1-35
Thursday	Closed doors, open doors	Acts 16:6-10, 2 Corinthians 2:12
Friday	Listening or resisting?	Acts 21:8-14
Saturday	The family likeness	Romans 8:14, 28-30

SMALL GROUP EXERCISE

(See *Celebrating the Disciplines: A Journal Workbook to Accompany Celebration of Discipline*, pp. 59, 60.)

Discerning Discernment

The following two exercises are designed to help you reflect on the Discipline of guidance in your own life. After completing the following two activities, discuss your responses with the group.

1 In the columns below, write down your thoughts about the unique strengths and liabilities of seeking God's guidance in community versus seeking it individually.

	Strengths	Liabilities
Seeking God's guidance in community	_____	_____
	_____	_____
	_____	_____
	_____	_____
Seeking God's guidance individually	_____	_____
	_____	_____
	_____	_____
	_____	_____

② Check your level of comfort or discomfort with the following forms of spiritual direction and guidance.

	Very Comfortable	Somewhat Comfortable	Not Sure	Somewhat Uncomfortable	Very Uncomfortable
A formally established community of believers, with clearly structured organization and authority	☐	☐	☐	☐	☐
An informally gathered community of believers, with spontaneous and fluid lines of organization and authority	☐	☐	☐	☐	☐
A spiritual director	☐	☐	☐	☐	☐
A network of trusted friends with common commitments and shared beliefs	☐	☐	☐	☐	☐
Preaching	☐	☐	☐	☐	☐
Small group ministry	☐	☐	☐	☐	☐
Bible reading and study	☐	☐	☐	☐	☐

INDIVIDUAL EXERCISES

To better discern the voice of God, ask yourself the following seven questions after you feel that you have heard him speak.*

Thoughts

1. *Does it sound like God?*

Does what you heard sound like something God would say? Is it consistent with God as you know him through Scripture?

2. *Does it sound like Jesus Christ?*

Does it sound like something Jesus would say? Is it consistent with Jesus as you see him revealed in the pages of the New Testament?

3. *Is it consistent with the overarching themes of Scripture?*

God's spoken Word will not contradict his written Word.

Emotions

4. *Is the emotional impact consistent with the fruit of the Spirit? After the communication, did I experience increased love, peace, and joy or just the opposite of these?*

The fruit of the Spirit is the character of Christ and associated with the emotions of abundant life.

Will

5. *Does it help me be conformed to the image of Christ?*

The glory of God is our transformation into Christlikeness.

Behavior

6. *Is it consistent with a previous experience I have had that I now know was from God?*

We can take advantage of the 20-20 vision of hindsight.

Social Interactions

7. *Do my closest friends and spiritual mentors believe it was from God?*

Do I get a witness from those I trust?

*This list of questions is from a longer list developed by Marty Goehring as part of a lecture on practical discernment.

Teaching Outline

BEFORE YOU LEAD: (TIPS FOR FACILITATOR)

I. INTRODUCTION (WELCOME/PRAYER)

II. WARM-UP (OVERVIEW/FREEDOM/DISCUSSION)

III. DVD (VIDEO/TRUTHS/RESPONSE/REFLECTION)

IV. BIBLE STUDY (INSIGHT/EXERCISE/MEDITATION)

V. EXERCISES (GROUP AND INDIVIDUAL)

VI. SUMMARY (RECOMMENDATIONS/RESOURCES)

Notes

_____

_____

_____

_____

_____

_____

_____

_____

_____

_____

_____

_____

_____

_____

_____

_____

SESSION THIRTEEN:
Celebration

BEFORE YOU LEAD

■ Quotes and Quips

The Christian should be an alleluia from head to foot!

Augustine of Hippo

I know what it means to be "God-intoxicated."

Frank Laubach

Joy comes through obedience to Christ, and joy results from obedience to Christ. Without obedience, joy is hollow and artificial.

Richard J. Foster

Celebration stands at the end of our study because joy is the end result of the Spiritual Disciplines' having functioned in our lives. God brings about the transformation of our lives through the Disciplines, and not until there is a transforming work within us do we know genuine joy.

Richard J. Foster

■ Key Scriptures

Our mouth was filled with laughter, and our tongue with shouts of joy....

Psalm 126:2a (NRSV)

Get the fatted calf and kill it, and let us eat and celebrate; for this son of mine was dead and is alive again....

Luke 15:23, 24

Jumping up, he stood and began to walk, and he entered the temple with them, walking and leaping and praising God.

Acts 3:8

...Jesus the pioneer and perfecter of our faith, who for the sake of the joy that was set before him endured the cross....

Hebrews 12:2

■ Note to Leader

If you are using the one-page lesson outlines, you will want to locate that page in the appendix to this lesson or on the CD-ROM now. Please continue to select from the menu of options provided in constructing a lesson tailored to the needs of your group.

SESSION OUTLINE

I. INTRODUCTION
- ■ Welcome
- ■ Prayer

II. WARM-UP
- ■ Overview/Illustration
- ■ Corresponding Freedom
- ■ Discussion of Homework

III. DVD
- ■ Video Vignette
- ■ Central Truths
- ■ Class Response
- ■ Reflection Questions

IV. BIBLE STUDY
- ■ Leader's Insight
- ■ Group Exercise
- ■ Scripture Meditation

V. EXERCISES FOR...
- ■ Small Group Exercise
- ■ Individual Exercises:
  - • Thoughts • Emotions • Will
  - • Behavior • Social Interactions

VI. SUMMARY
- ■ Richard's Recommendations
- ■ Other RENOVARÉ Resources

■ Materials

For this session *the leader* will need:

- ■ Leader's Guide
- ■ Bible
- ■ DVD Player, Monitor, Stand, Extension Cord, etc.
- ■ *Celebration of Discipline* DVD
- ■ *Celebration of Discipline* (Chapter 13)

For this session *the participant* will need:

- ■ Bible
- ■ Participant's Guide
- ■ Pen or Pencil

INTRODUCTION

■ Welcome

Call your group together and welcome the participants to session thirteen of *Celebration of Discipline*. Our Discipline for this time together is celebration.

■ Prayer
(see http://www.communityofhopeinc.org/Prayer%20Pages/Saints/augustine.html)

PRAYER OF JOY AT THE BIRTH OF JESUS

Let the just rejoice,
for their Justifict is born.
Let the sick and infirm rejoice,
for their Savior is born.
Let captives rejoice,
for their Redeemer is born.
Let slaves rejoice,
for their Master is born.
Let free people rejoice,
for their Liberator is born.
Let all Christians rejoice,
for Jesus Christ is born.

Saint Augustine of Hippo

Warm-Up

■ Overview and Illustration

Celebration is at the beginning and the end of the journey of spiritual formation. It is the hope of joy that rightfully motivates a person to begin the practice of Spiritual Disciplines, and it is the experience of joy that signals a growing friendship with God.

But how does this journey work? What is the model for change?

Imagine a person who is free to enjoy playing the piano—perhaps you are that person. The freedom to play with grace and delight was not always present. There was a time in her life when she could not play. But either the person or her parent had a hope-filled *vision* for what it would be like for her to play beautifully. The vision provided motivation for the *intention*—a will to learn—to be birthed. And with the proper *means*—lessons and practice sessions—she eventually learned to play. With time and disciplined practice, great freedom and joy were realized.

Whether the goal is to learn to play a musical instrument, to learn a new language, or to stop being an addict, the general pattern for personal transformation is the same. And it applies to spiritual formation as well (see *Renovation of the Heart: Putting On the Character of Christ*, pp. 85-89). To help keep this general pattern in mind, Richard Foster and Dallas Willard use the acronym VIM, as in the phrase "vim and vigor." Let's look at the three components a bit more closely:

Vision is the ability to see what may not already exist. In the context of Christian spiritual formation, vision refers to seeing ourselves transformed and living in God's kingdom—*joyfully* conformed to the image of Christ. A vision of joy motivated Christ to endure the cross (Hebrews 12:2), and joy motivates a person to begin the path of authentic transformation that leads to taking on the character of Christ (see also *Renovation of the Heart: Leader's Guide*, pp. 101-111).

Intention is a resolve or determination to act in a certain way. In the context of Christian spiritual formation, it means *intending* to realize the vision of being like Jesus. The vision of a joyful life with Christ provides the motivation that shapes a person's will to pursue the means of change.

Means are the methods and resources for accomplishing something. The teachings of Christ found in Scripture, classic

devotional writings, invoking the power and presence of Jesus in our lives, and *the practice of Christian Disciplines* are means of authentic Christian transformation.

And what is the end result of the VIM model as applied to Christian formation? Joyous celebration! In the words of Richard Foster:

> That is why I have placed celebration at the end of this study. Joy is the end result of the Spiritual Disciplines' functioning in our lives. God brings about the transformation of our lives through the Disciplines, and we will not know genuine joy until there is a transforming work within us. (*Celebration of Discipline*, p. 193)

Given that Jesus stated that he came to earth to bring life, more abundant life (see John 10:10), it only makes sense that celebration bookends the process of Christian formation.

■ Corresponding Freedom

Celebration brings transformation of character and friendship with God.

■ Homework Check-Up

If your group has decided to read the corresponding chapters of *Celebration of Discipline* and participate in the daily Scripture readings or transforming exercises as outside-of-class activities, this is the time to do an accountability check and ask for comments concerning the experiences of any participants who would like to share.

 D V D

■ Video

In the first segment of this video presentation, Richard Foster provides an introduction to the Discipline of celebration. He is assisted through a discussion with Glandion Carney and Margaret Campbell.

If your group desires, you can let the DVD continue through a second segment called "Soul Talk" and listen in on a conversation between Richard and Dallas Willard.

■ **Central Truths** (pp. 102, 103 in Participant's Guide)

You are provided with a few summary points for the teaching section of each video vignette. Here are the Central Truths for the video session about celebration.

- The acronym **VIM** provides for us the bigger picture or backdrop as we talk about our final Discipline, celebration.
   - ◆ **V is for Vision.**
     For Christian spiritual formation to work, we need a vision for life in the kingdom of God and a sense of what Jesus meant when he said, "I've come that you might have life and have it more abundantly."

   - ◆ **I is for Intention.**
     Intention is the clarity of direction for where we are going and for having arrival there as our explicit purpose. Intention is saying, "I have decided to follow Jesus."

   - ◆ **M is for Means.**
     The means are the Disciplines of the spiritual life that lead us forward so that we might grow in grace.

- Celebration is one of the loveliest of the Spiritual Disciplines.

- Celebration stands at the end of our study because joy is the end result of the Spiritual Disciplines.

- When the destructive habits—our automatic responses against the kingdom—in our lives have been conquered, it is joy!

- "The spirit of hurry and the spirit of joy do not reside in the same house." (Evelyn Underhill)

- We need to discover ways to celebrate, perhaps by beginning with the great festivals of worship in Scripture.

- Other occasions to celebrate may include celebrating when a

life has been changed (e.g., a drug addiction conquered or a marriage restored); celebrating and redeeming the festivals of our culture (e.g., Halloween as a festival for the great saints of the church, or Thanksgiving and Christmas); and our own occasions for celebration (e.g., family vacations and rites of passage such as birthdays, graduations, weddings, and anniversaries).

■ In celebration we also see the other Disciplines come into play—such as submitting to others' ideas about what constitutes a celebration, or celebrating as the natural expression of our joy in receiving forgiveness.

■ Class Response

Do you have any questions or observations about the video vignettes before we look at the Reflection Questions together?

■ Reflection Questions (p. 103 in Participant's Guide)

Video: Lecture

1 How does the Discipline of celebration fit within the VIM model?

2 When is the last time you felt like "an alleluia from head to foot"? Was your celebration contagious?

3 Why does Richard place celebration at the end of his list of Spiritual Disciplines?

4 What is one way you can add more celebration to your life next week?

Book (See *Study Guide for Celebration of Discipline*, p. 74.)

1 Do you enjoy God?

2 Why do you think human beings often find celebration so difficult?

3 How about planning a family, nonholiday celebration this year?

At the close of this study, what covenant *must* you make with the Lord?

BIBLE STUDY

If time permits, form small groups and allow the participants to complete the Bible study exercise in class.

■ Group Exercise

We will now turn our attention to the Bible as a frame of reference. A brief Bible study can be found on pages 104, 105 in the Participant's Guide and may be used in class or as a homework assignment.

■ Leader's Insight

Participant's Guide p. 104

The Bible provides a potpourri of passages about celebration. As Richard Foster states in the lead sentence to his chapter on this Discipline, "Celebration is at the heart of the way of Christ" (p. 190).

■ John the Baptist leaped for joy in Elizabeth's womb upon hearing Mary's voice (Luke 1:41).

■ Angels announced Jesus' birth with shouts of joy (Luke 2:10).

■ Jesus began his public ministry with the promise of good news, freedom, and liberation (Luke 4:18, 19).

■ He stated that the purpose of his coming was to provide abundant life (John 10:10).

■ He endured the cross for the *joy* set before him (Hebrews 12:2).

■ Jesus left the world bequeathing his joy to the disciples: "These things I have spoken to you, that my joy may be in you, and that your joy may be made full" (John 15:11, NASB)

But even with all these passages to ponder, the most indelible image of Jesus' focus on joy and celebration may be found in the fact that he used a seven-day wedding feast as the backdrop for his first public miracle. Consider the following reflections on John 2:1-10 (from *Falling for God*, pp. 20, 21).

Jesus has had a lot of time to think about the moment of his first miracle. He waited a very long time after the Fall before stepping into human history, and then waited thirty more years before beginning his public ministry: millennia to consider this moment, the event of his first miracle.

Surely it was no accident that he chose a wedding feast as the occasion—after all, the church will come to be referred to as his bride, and he the groom. But there seems to be something else going on here, something symbolic, mystical. No surprise that John, the mystic, is the only Gospel writer to cover this breaking story. Jesus asks for six earthen vessels containing twenty to thirty gallons of water. A gallon of water weighs in at about seven pounds. Earthen vessels, containing mostly water, weighing between 140 and 210 pounds. That describes most of the people I know.

With wedding images in the background, Jesus takes center stage and kicks off his public ministry by radically changing the contents of earthen vessels. Spirit is added, and plain water becomes extraordinary wine. Transformation. Jesus' first miracle foreshadows all that will follow. It's about radical changes to the contents of earthen vessels. Water to wine. Saul to Paul. You to Jesus. Now *that*— having the contents of our earthen vessels radically transformed by mystical union with Christ—is something to celebrate!

■ Scripture Meditation

Please note that the Bible Study also includes suggestions for daily Scripture readings (p. 105 in Participant's Guide). Encourage the group participants to spend five to ten minutes with these passages of Scripture each day. As you progress through these sessions, the participants may want to expand this time frame and use these daily passages as part of *lectio divina*.

TRANSFORMING EXERCISES

Please see pages 106-108 in the Participant's Guide to observe the suggested *Small Group Exercise* and *Individual Exercises*. The *Small Group Exercise* is typically designed for use during your session together. The *Individual Exercises* are based on Dallas Willard's five components of the person and are constructed for the participants to use as homework activities.

SMALL GROUP

Participant's Guide p. 106

INDIVIDUAL

Participant's Guide p. 108

SUMMARY

■ Review

The Christian Disciplines are practices and attitudes of the heart that help a person become more open to God's grace. As the subtitle of *Celebration of Discipline* suggests, Christian Discipline is "the path to spiritual growth." Christian maturity is the process of transformation in which our entire person (thoughts, emotions, will, behaviors, and social interactions) becomes more like Christ. And as we journey on this path with God, our acquaintance with him deepens into apprenticeship and then into friendship. Taking on the character of Christ and becoming his friend are the cause of our most joyous and free-spirited celebration!

■ Richard's Recommendations

Something old: *The Christian's Secret of a Happy Life* by
Hannah Whitall Smith, 1832-1911. (New
Kensington, PA: Whitaker House, 1983)

Something new: *A Tree Full of Angels* by Macrina
Wiederkehr. (San Francisco
HarperSanFrancisco, 1990)

■ Other RENOVARÉ Resources

Celtic Daily Prayer compiled by the Northumbria Community.
(San Francisco: HarperSanFrancisco, 2002)

APPENDIX

Use the appendix that follows to facilitate class exercises and
homework. The *Bible Study, Small Group Exercise*, and *Individual
Exercises* can be found in the Participant's Guide.

Bible Study and Daily Bible Readings
Transforming Exercises (Group and Individual)
Teaching Outline

BIBLE STUDY

Read John 2:1-10.

1 Do you think it is significant that Jesus chose a wedding for the setting of his first miracle? How so?

2 Do you believe the miracle of Cana also foreshadows the sacrament of Holy Communion? (Hint: How does Communion symbolize the mystery of "Christ in me" and changing the contents of earthen vessels?)

3 Does the content of your earthen vessel seem more like water or wine right now? Why, and what can you do to help bring about a change—or continue to be brimming with the good stuff?

4 What events in your journey with Jesus have been cause for celebration?

Daily Scripture Readings

(from *Study Guide for Celebration of Discipline*, p. 73)

Day	Theme	Passage
Sunday	The Lord has triumphed gloriously	Exodus 15:1-2, 20-21
Monday	The joy of the Lord	2 Samuel 6:12-19
Tuesday	Bless the Lord	Psalm 103
Wednesday	Praise the Lord	Psalm 150
Thursday	Hosanna!	Luke 19:35-40 John 12:12-19
Friday	Walking and leaping and praising God	Acts 3:1-10
Saturday	Hallelujah!	Revelation 19:1-8

S M A L L   G R O U P   E X E R C I S E

(See *Celebrating the Disciplines: A Journal Workbook to Accompany Celebration of Discipline*, pp. 194, 195.)

Celebrating Celebration

Suggestion #1: Scripture Passages Relevant to the Practice of Celebration

Take a few moments to search for your favorite passage of Scripture that calls us to the joyful living made possible through the life, death, and resurrection of Christ. After everyone in the group locates the passage, allow each willing participant to share an overview of the selection and explain why it is a favorite.

Hint: If anyone needs direction, the following passages are of particular relevance:

Exodus 15:1-21	Celebration of deliverance
2 Samuel 6:1-23	A call to obedience and participation in a rejoicing community
Luke 4:18-19	Jesus announces his ministry
John 2:1-11	A special wedding feast
John 15:11	Jesus' desire for our joy
Galatians 5:22-23	Evidence of transformation
Hebrews 12:1-3	Joy as a powerful motivator for Jesus

Suggestion #2:   Throwing a Party in God's Honor

Take some time for your group to organize a party to celebrate the experience of practicing Christian Disciplines and the joy of getting to know one another. As you plan, you may want to consider the following ideas:

- ◼ A loosely structured gathering for spontaneous conversation

- ◼ A potluck dinner party with each person bringing a favorite dish and something from his or her home that reveals a personal interest

- ◼ A meal organized around a seasonal or holiday theme

I N D I V I D U A L   E X E R C I S E S

(See *Celebrating the Disciplines: A Journal Workbook to Accompany Celebration of Discipline,* pp. 67, 68, 192.)

Thoughts

Interview a person who is a living celebration. Ask for the secret to his or her joyous living, and take plenty of notes.

Emotions

In a small group setting, have people tell their funniest stories from past church activities and experiences.

Will

In what areas of your life is it hardest for you to choose to place carefree trust in God's ability to meet all your needs? After answering this question, enter into dialogue with God and ask him to help you be more able to embrace this freedom from anxiety.

Behavior

Are there any ways in which specific and repeated acts of disobedience have robbed you of joy? Make a list and share it with God (and perhaps a trusted friend). Pray for the grace of increased obedience and friendship with God.

Social Interactions

Get together with one or more friends sometime this week simply for relaxation and pleasure. Celebrate the simple goodness of life: find a place to play, and then lose yourself in fun; watch a funny movie; mock your own seriousness; tell silly jokes; have a good laugh.

108   C E L E B R A T I O N   O F   D I S C I P L I N E

Teaching Outline

BEFORE YOU LEAD: (TIPS FOR FACILITATOR)

I. INTRODUCTION (WELCOME/PRAYER)

II. WARM-UP (OVERVIEW/FREEDOM/DISCUSSION)

III. DVD (VIDEO/TRUTHS/RESPONSE/REFLECTION)

IV. BIBLE STUDY (INSIGHT/EXERCISE/MEDITATION)

V. EXERCISES (GROUP AND INDIVIDUAL)

VI. SUMMARY (RECOMMENDATIONS/RESOURCES)

List of Works Cited

Adler, Mortimer J. *How to Read a Book*. New York: Simon & Schuster, 1940.

Bonhoeffer, Dietrich. *Life Together*. San Francisco: Harper and Row, 1954.

The Book of Common Prayer. New York: The Church Hymnal Corporation, 1979.

Celebration of Discipline Video Series. Victory Films, Worcester, Pennsylvania, 1984.

Crim, Keith R., Victor P. Furnish and Lloyd R. Bailey, eds. *The Interpreter's Dictionary of the Bible*. Abingdon Press, 1976.

Foster, Richard J. *Celebration of Discipline: The Path to Spiritual Growth* (25th Anniversary Edition). San Francisco: HarperSanFrancisco, 2003.

_____ and Emilie Griffin, eds. *Spiritual Classics: Selected Readings for Individuals and Groups on the Twelve Spiritual Disciplines*. SanFrancisco: HarperSanFrancisco, 2000.

_____. *Freedom of Simplicity*. San Francisco: Harper & Row, 1981.

_____ and Kathryn A. Yanni. *Celebrating the Disciplines: A Journal Workbook to Accompany Celebration of Discipline*. San Francisco: HarperSanFrancisco, 1992.

_____. *Meditative Prayer*. Downers Grove, Illinois: InterVarsity Press, 1983.

_____. *Prayer: Finding the Heart's True Home*. San Francisco: HarperSanFranciso, 1992.

_____. *Prayers From the Heart*. San Francisco: HarperSanFrancisco, 1994.

_____, ed. *The RENOVARÉ Spiritual Formation Bible*. San Francisco: HarperSanFrancisco, 2005.

_____. *Study Guide for Celebration of Discipline*. San Francisco: HarperSanFrancisco, 1983.

http://bible.crosswalk.com/Commentaries/JamiesonFaussetBrown/jfb.cgi

http://www.catholic.net/hope_healing/template_channel.phtml?channel_id=22

http:// www.communityofhopeinc.org/Prayer%20Pages/Saints/augustine.html

"An Introduction to the Practice of Lectio Divina," www.valyermo.com/ld-art.html

Kelly, Thomas R. *A Testament of Devotion*. San Francisco: HarperSanFrancisco, 1992.

Lucado, Max and Ron DiCianni. *Tell Me the Secrets*. Wheaton, Illinois: Crossway Books, 1993.

Moon, Gary W. *Falling for God*. Colorado Springs: WaterBrook Press, 2004.

_____. *Renovation of the Heart: Leader's Guide*. Franklin Springs, Georgia: LifeSprings Resources, 2003.

NIV Study Bible. Grand Rapids, Michigan: Zondervan Publishing House, 1995.

Nouwen, Henri. *Out of Solitude*. Notre Dame, Indiana: Ave Maria Press, 1974.

Plantinga, Jr., Cornelius. *Not the Way It's Supposed to Be: A Breviary of Sin*. Grand Rapids, Michigan: Wm. B. Eerdmans Publishing Co., 1995.

Sanford, Agnes. *The Healing Light*. New York: Ballantine Books, 1983.

Smedes, Lewis. *Union With Christ*. Grand Rapids, Michigan: Wm. B. Eerdmans Publishing Co., 1983.

Temple, Gray. *The Molten Soul: Dangers and Opportunities in Religious Conversion*. New York: Church Publishing, Inc., 2000.

Willard, Dallas. *The Divine Conspiracy: Rediscovering Our Hidden Life in God*. San Francisco: HarperCollins, 1998.

_____. *Hearing God: Developing a Conversational Relationship With God*. Downers Grove, Illinois: InterVarsity Press, 1999.

_____. *Renovation of the Heart: Putting On the Character of Christ*. Colorado Springs: NavPress, 2002.

_____. *The Spirit of the Disciplines: Understanding How God Changes Lives*. San Francisco: HarperSanFrancisco, 1988.